Death
of a
Fairy Tale

Claiming the Happier Ever After...Divorce

Death
of a
Fairy Tale

Claiming the Happier Ever After...Divorce

D. L. Mars

Unless otherwise noted, all Scriptures are taken from the *Holy Bible, New International Version*, Copyright © 1973, 1978, 1984 by the International Bible Society. Used by permission of Zondervan Publishing House.

Scripture taken from the *New King James Version*. Copyright © 1982 by Thomas Nelson, Inc. Used by permission. All rights reserved.

Scripture references marked niv are taken from the Holy Bible, New International Version, Copyright © 1973, 1978, 1984 by the International Bible Society. Used by permission of Zondervan Publishing House. The "niv" and "New International Version" trademarks are registered in the United States Patent and Trademark Office by International Bible Society.

Printing in the United States
10 9 8 7 6 5 4 3 2 1

Library of Congress Catalog Card Number: 2012941561

For more information or to contact the author, please go to:
www.DeathOfAFairyTale.com

This life work is dedicated to my phenomenal children, Alex and Zoe. You are my inspiration, my bookends, my wind.

Thank you for dispelling the myth that kids from "broken homes" have broken wings. I will always cherish you and each moment we have the privilege to share together.

Contents

Foreword

Tales of the courageous deserve to be told. Author D. L. Mars does just that in this brilliant book, *Death of a Fairy Tale.*

More than seven years ago, D. L. shared her vision for this book with me. She wanted to provide women with a universal and safe environment in which to confront their debilitating marital pain. She wanted them to embrace healing faster than she did. She envisioned that the collective stories from other sojourners would leave a trail of bread crumbs for those who, like Dorothy in *The Wizard of Oz* or *Little Red Riding Hood* after encountering the big bad wolf, were having trouble finding their way back home.

But D. L. Mars's ambition does not stop with the villains who destroy marriages. In the chapter "Setting Royal Standards," she uses literary license and her own life experience to help women who are contemplating marriage map out a trustworthy route that will hopefully lead them to a long-lasting and rewarding relationship. She shows them how to avoid a tragic ending by providing clear suggestions and thoughtful questions to consider before you say, "I do."

What do courageous women have to do with fairy tales? Truth and self-reliance. D. L. Mars weaves together the authentic and often tragic stories of women who thought they were entering a fairy tale marriage or relationship. At some point, each summoned the strength to tap the power within to rescue herself from a bad situation.

As a counselor, mother, and wife of thirty-two years, I have seen, heard, and experienced the devastation of women who are unable or unwilling to determine the necessary questions that need to be asked prior to committing to a relationship. I have found that some women are so broken by past experiences that they do not understand that just because something looks good to you does not mean that it is good for you.

This wonderful book encourages the reader to do many things, including establishing intimacy with yourself, determining where you are so you have a better view of where you are going, and seeking early intervention when necessary. Determining where you are in your life can help you know if you are near the edge of a cliff or five minutes away from the desired destination. I have found few helpful road maps in life, but I do consider D. L. Mars's book just that. I am in complete agreement with her thesis that it is never too late to assess, adjust, and then progress toward your destiny.

Establishing intimacy with oneself is difficult but imperative. It requires discipline (a willingness to keep working) and authenticity (a desire to get to one's truth). D. L. Mars, through examples of her own life story and divorce along with the tales of other women who are empowered by truth, provides some clear strategies for how others can learn to embrace and validate themselves.

Death of a Fairy Tale is highly recommended for all women. For women who are mesmerized by a "fantasy" in the beginning, stuck in the middle, living in bliss, or at the ending of a once-promising relationship and having difficulty determining the next steps, *Death of a Fairy Tale* (along with counseling, support groups, or other traditional interventions) can certainly be a significant part of healing.

I never understood why Humpty Dumpty sat on the wall. Had he not properly assessed his situation? Had he not been honest with himself about the height of the wall? Did he always think that if he fell, someone would come to his aid? Well, we know that at the end of the fairy tale, Humpty Dumpty could not be put back together again. This book helps you avoid a fatal fall like Humpty Dumpty's. I encourage you to let D. L. Mars help you edit your own story in a way that allows you to embrace life with integrity and honesty, in a way that will ensure that you live in the reality of what it takes to get to the happily ever after.

—Rev. Dr. Lael C. Melville
Family therapist, CORE
(Consistently Operating in Reality for Eternity)

Acknowledgments
A Note of Gratitude and Celebration

In **Memory** of my loving parents and protectors, Quentin Mars, Sr. and Lozella Mars. Your marriage dignified the meaning of "Till death do us part." I am honored to carry forth your legacy and will do so as long as there is breath in me. Also in memory of my brother, Quentin Mars II—Who I am sure is keeping heaven lively! And Marshilia E. Snoddy my forever friend who earned the title: Queen of the Road you are forever in my heart.

In Honor of every single mother who has put her life on pause to raise her children. Keep pushing, keep dreaming, love yourself, and know when it is necessary to say "enough."

Thank You:

To my big sister, Carrye Mars-Baker, for believing in me and for praying for me always.

To my godmother, Evelyn B. Thornton, for your unconditional love and support through the years.

To the hundreds of women who generously shared their stories with me: Thank you on behalf of all the readers who will be blessed and empowered by your individual and collective journey. Never give up on yourself or on life. My prayer is that each of you will experience a Ruth and Boaz kind of love one day. In the meantime, continue to live in truth and consistently commit to self-love and care.

To my brilliant subject matter experts: Carla Beene, Esq., Dr. Yolanda Brooks, Rev. Lucretia Facen, Dr. Phyllis Gee, Rev. Joyce Kitchen, Ms. Theresa Little, Mr. Rick Lindsey, Dr. Lael Melville, Elder Cathy Moffit, Dr. Sheila Peters, and Dr. Tracy Shaw, along with the many others who enlightened me along the way. I know that your wisdom will uplift and educate the masses.

To My Royal Court: Athena Dean Holtz and the entire Redemption Press Team, Jamacia Johnson and Mark Hill (Graphic Artists), Caroline Wilkins (Researcher) each of you have demonstrated a commitment to excellence by bringing your gifts and talents to this project and for this I am grateful.

To my Prince of Peace, my Lifeguard, my Healer, and my Creator. I give all praise, glory, and honor to God for allowing me the privilege to carry forth this difficult and controversial topic. It is only by your grace that I have triumphed over the sting of divorce. It is only by your love that I feel loveable again. It is only by your mercy that I have the ability to find joy in each and every day again. Thank you for giving me a second chance to reclaim my life.

The stories told in the following chapters
are all based on true events.

Names have been changed to protect
the women who lived them.

"The greatest gift you will ever receive is the gift of loving and believing in yourself. Guard this gift with your life. It is the only thing that will ever truly be yours."
—Tiffany Loren Rowe

I leaned back in my seat as the plane soared over the ocean. I was tanned and relaxed, returning from a much-deserved vacation in Cancun after completing what I thought was the final manuscript for this book. Suddenly and without warning, the cabin filled with smoke. I found myself gasping for air. As the flight attendants instructed passengers to drop to the floor and cover our heads, I was consumed by the numbing fear that this was really the end of my life.

My mind shot to the image of my children at my funeral. Then it raced to my brother's and my mother's funerals. "God, am I going to die tragically like them?"

I became consumed with all of the lives I carried with me both in my heart and on my hard drive. After being emotionally dead for over thirty years, I had a message to share, a purpose I had not yet completed. Dying on this plane on this day was not an option.

Introduction

Chosen

My Brother's Keeper

"**D**ebbie, are you sure you want to go in?"
I replied, "Yes, Mama 2, I am going in with you. I don't want Mommy and Daddy to have to deal with this."I was lying to my brother's godmother and myself. Although I was considered mature for my age, I was not prepared to be an adult that day. But I was here now, so no turning back. An unfamiliar coldness sent tremors through my body as I tried to calm my nerves when the tech asked us if we were ready.

I was expecting stainless steel refrigerated compartments to line the walls just like I had seen on TV. Without warning, an oversized picture of my brother was projected on a huge screen. I felt my legs buckle. I wanted to run. What was I thinking? What sixteen-year-old in their "right" mind volunteers to go to the morgue?

A few days later, when they closed the lid on his casket, the joy that had once been my family's hallmark got buried too. Childhood was officially over for me.

Before this tragedy, the summer of 1973 had been brimming with typical teen activity like trips to the beach, sneaking to house parties in neighborhoods that were not sanctioned by our parents, shopping for the hippest wardrobe for *Soul Train*, and everything in between.

Even though I had completed my graduation requirements at the end of my junior year, I'd decided to hang around one more year so I could fully embrace senior privileges. I couldn't wait to participate in ditch day, snatch night, and prom. I was also about to become a debutante. My mom and I were having a blast poring over fabrics and designing my debutante dress and thinking ahead about my prom ensemble. She was a very gifted self-taught seamstress. I could only imagine what she would come up with when it was time for me to get married one day.

"Which one of these artists is your favorite, Brother?" I asked as I watched an infectious smile spread across his face.

My big brother, "Brother," took me back and forth to my evening debutante rehearsals in his turquoise blue Impala with the black rag top. He loved that car so much. I loved to watch his big Afro bouncing to the sounds of Chicago, The Dramatics, Roberta Flack, and Jimi Hendrix, all of whom always seemed to be blasting in the car.

"I love them all," he said with a laugh, as he turned up the volume. Those animated exchanges suddenly became memories that I desperately wanted to snatch from death's grip as I stood there viewing his lifeless body.

Scared to Death

Just like Mommy and Daddy, I became quite good at becoming an enviable survivor of just about anything life threw my way. On the outside I was confident, funny, and cool as a cucumber; and on the inside I was a raging inferno of emotions—certain that tragedy would strike again. And this hypothesis became a predictable self-fulfilling prophecy.

Mommy spent her last ten years of life after Brother's death inwardly grieving the loss of her only son and then that of her mother around the five-year anniversary of his death. We were told that my grandmother was robbed and her house set afire with her in it. My mother paced the hallway of Parkland Memorial Hospital's burn ward in Dallas, Texas, for six weeks until my Grandma Rita took her painful last breath.

Through it all, Mommy remained prayerful and selfless. Even when she found herself battling a very aggressive form of breast cancer multiple times, she found the strength to help raise my nieces Kim and Sydney after my sister and their father divorced. I know in my heart that while her death certificate stated complications from cancer, Mommy died a premature death because of a broken heart.

Even though she never witnessed my wedding day or the birth of my children, I am grateful that she got to witness the launch of my career.

"Debbie, I want you to take that job," she whispered. Frito Lay is a good company and I know you will be successful there. Take the job, Baby."

Even on her deathbed, while in and out of consciousness, she was still loving and instructing me to accept a job offer at Frito Lay in Dallas.

The next day, when she died after her seven-year battle, I was barely twenty-six years old and suddenly motherless. After her funeral, I went back to Houston, resigned from Coca-Cola, and dutifully headed down the road to Dallas, to Frito

Lay. Just like her, I did not stop to grieve. I just charged in like a gladiator who had just stepped foot into an arena of chaos.

When I arrived at the chip maker's ivory towers in Exchange Park, Debra the warrior took over. Like Sleeping Beauty, Debbie was laid to rest for a very long time.

It turns out I was trail blazing as the first African American female marketing executive at Frito Lay. In addition to being on the launch team of Chester Cheetah (Cheetos' hip spokescat), I led Doritos into the Spring Break College Market and created numerous award-winning national promotions—including Super Bowl and the Grandma's Cookies Mystery Shopper. While I tamed my grief by channeling my creative gene, my soul sat empty on a shelf.

As I left the doctor's office, other than shocked, I didn't know how to feel. There were surges of both joy and fear battling for my attention. My doctor's words cut through my warrior mentality and exposed my feminine softness; my inner core . . . without my permission.

"You're going to have a baby," he said. I wasn't sure how to feel, but Debra the warrior could handle this and everything else that came her way all while never letting on that she was scared to death and petrified of failure.

As I processed my options in the first trimester, I would run three floors down the back stairwell just so I could throw up in a bathroom where I was not as well known by co-workers.

Being a single parent in the 1980s was taboo—especially in the corporate world—and even more so for a high-profile black woman. The pregnancy created an almost unbearable tension in my relationship with my child's father and it also drove a temporary wedge between my father and me.

"So, how are you going to handle this?" My father's words and change in attitude biased my volatile thoughts about motherhood. Even though it was unplanned and unwanted, thinking of a baby was the first time my heart attempted to smile since all the death that had overtaken my thoughts for over a decade. I was very conflicted. Had she been alive, Mommy would have helped me make sense of all this and would have defended me against this world.

Temporarily, I felt completely orphaned and left to fend for my baby and me. Panicked, I did what I did best—I became more ambitious than ever to prove that professionaly I was still relevant even with a baby bump. The senior executives were surprisingly very supportive—probably because of my performance track record, but many peers, and even subordinates, turned out to be workplace bullies.

Instead of focusing on nurturing a healthy pregnancy, I focused on how to minimize the rumor mill. Once I made the decision to keep the baby, the pregnancy was the loneliest and most humiliating time of my life to date.

I realize now that there is no time more sacred to a woman than a pregnancy—regardless of marital status or external support. However, I allowed antagonists, including my son's father, to rob me of a sacred journey that I will never have again.

But just before my son's second birthday, something happened that I did not expect.

Cross It Off the Bucket List

"Will you marry me?" These were words I'd longed to hear all my life and especially once I found myself unexpectedly pregnant. My baby's father had orchestrated an elaborate and surprise proposal that was difficult to deny. Without thinking I dismissed all the hurt and humiliation he had caused me for over 2 years. Had I been thinking I would have asked the question "why now"? When he proposed, we weren't even dating. In fact I was in a very serious and loving relationship with a man who wanted to marry me and adopt my young son. As powerful as the business world had endorsed that I was and even having someone in my life who loved me for me, all along I had felt secretly demoralized and now pathetically grateful that finally I had been chosen by my baby's father.

I packed away the single parent stigma along with my pride and began planning a society wedding that my mother, the Queen of Style would have been very proud of. "This color is fabulous! Magic is my middle name" I mumbled to myself as I viewed my wedding storyboard that displayed the pastel color swatches for my bridesmaids.

My inherited gifts to beautify and entertain – just like my mother – proved very effective during my wedding planning. I call it Fairy Dusting. Unfortunately, just like my mother, those aesthetic distractions delayed the healing process and the reality that for two years I had been rejected by my new fiancé. We spent about an hour with our minister more so to receive his blessing. We needed premarital counseling in the worse way.

My father paid for my hand beaded dress and reluctantly gave his blessings. He graciously let me make my own decision while I am sure, was crossing his fingers and holding his breath.

Now, I was making progress. I scratched the baby and marriage both off the bucket list – even if they were out of order. Being an entrepreneur had always loomed in the back of my mind because my father had mastered the art of having multiple revenue streams. So after we got married and as my corporate travel inched up in excess of 40%, I formally launched my promotions agency and became an entrepreneur so that I could spend more time at home and expand our family.

Unlike our son, our daughter was planned almost down to the moment of conception. As much as her birth enhanced our world, unfortunately, her addition to our family did not prove to be what we needed to survive. Even my Fairy Dust—designing a warm environment and hosting family-oriented dinner parties—could not save our otherwise volatile marriage. My divorce was sudden and the aftermath from it nearly buried me alive. I now classify it as one of my life's most treacherous and confidence-draining dragons.

Writing this book became a dragon-slaying weapon that rescued my sanity and saved my life. When it came time to order the first 1,000 books, I was shaking change out of my piggy bank to finance it. Real dreams are self-funded by sweat equity and/or cold cash; otherwise, they belong to someone else. When I held the first copy of *Death of a Fairy Tale* in my arms, it was as if a spell had been lifted.

In the chapters that follow, I will introduce you to other women who have earned the title of Dragon Slayer. Like mine, their lessons were hard learned and their paths often rocky. As we forge ahead, after the tragic endings of our once fairy tale-inspired marriages, I invite you to watch as new life blossoms. Each woman generously shares, in her authentic voice, the truth and beauty unleashed by the rare gift of raw honesty and open disclosure. This serves as an inspiration for us all.

What have I learned through this experience? I've learned and experienced firsthand that most divorces do not come about because of one poison apple. Sometimes, the one rotten apple spills over to the other fruits of our lives and before you know it, the barrel is not salvageable.

Let's begin this journey with my own story—where I learned some of my own hard lessons. In hindsight, I do not question that my marriage had to die in order for me to fully grow into myself. Nor do I deny the past or the hand that I had in creating it. I accepted my husband's proposal without choosing to question his motives or the obvious consequences. I silenced my spirit for eight years and learned that true love and happiness do not come in the form of a diamond ring and a dream house but always stem from first loving and trusting who we see in the mirror.

Together let us summon the courage to eulogize the pain of the past. When we do, we can finally allow it to rest in peace and embark on the business of reclaiming the lives we were destined to live.

PART I
Cause of Death

Debbie's Ark: My Story

"For I know the plans I have for you,"declares the Lord, "plans to prosper you and not to harm you, plans to give you a hope and a future."
—Jeremiah 29:11, NIV

My childhood home was situated right in the heart of historic Wellington Square in Los Angeles. My parents purchased it when they found out they were pregnant with me. When Daddy died in 1999, he had amassed a portfolio of property, with the crown jewel being the pink stucco family residence on Virginia Road.

Over the years, it had been the gathering place for our large circle of family and friends. My father always said, "Keep a roof over your head," because that is what his father had told all of his ten children. Their advice was not intended as a suggestion—it was a mandate.

I had built my first home at age twenty-three when I was single and working in Houston for Coca-Cola. So when my husband insisted that we rent so that he could invest in entrepreneurial ventures, his game plan seemed counter-intuitive to me. Like with everything else in our marriage that I disagreed with, I sucked it up and dealt with it by not dealing with it.

Finally, after six years of marriage, he agreed to build my dream house in an exclusive Dallas suburb. From drafting blueprints to finishing details, the construction project took about eighteen months, but to me it was worth it. Early on, I grew concerned about the mounting costs and sensed that we had overstepped our financial means, but my husband assured me that we could "pull it off."

"Pull it off?" That signaled a red flag with me, but I wanted that house so bad that I crossed my fingers and set my sights on the housewarming.

I visited the construction site almost every day. Even though I was being pulled in a lot of directions—running a sizeable business, managing our home, juggling the kids' extracurricular activities and then my volunteer work, I always found time to check in on my dream house. When I could, I had interior decorators visit me at my corporate offices so I could multitask.

We would spread out fabric swatches, paint chips, and door handles on my conference table. As we got closer to the closing, my calendar was filled with almost as many construction meetings as client meetings. I would often daydream about taking our little girl for leisurely walks around the nearby lake so that she could feed the geese and ducks. The neighbors on our cul-de-sac had lots of boys, all close to our son's age. The plan was to move in right before school started, and I had even worked out carpool logistics with the nearby private school mothers. Everything seemed to be working out perfectly.

Most thought the buttery yellow stucco exterior resembled an Italian villa in the hills of Tuscany. It reminded me of being home in Southern California which is where, deep down, I secretly longed to be. So much so that I even imported palm trees for the backyard. Our So Cal Villa featured a state-of-the-art gourmet kitchen, wine cellar, formal library, putting green, craft and sewing room, media room, and most important, my private closet with shelving for an embarrassingly large shoe and accessory collection. I had even designed a special parlor adjacent to our daughter's bedroom to display her expansive doll collection.

We jointly made a very large deposit at the beginning of construction. Midway through, my husband suddenly deferred all aesthetic decisions to me and excluded himself from meetings with the builder. His defense became, "It was my Dream House not his." If I asked him any financial questions pertaining to the project, he would become confrontational and evasive. Unknowingly, I became the pawn who would be pressed to deliver on his contractual breaches that included our installment payments being late and a need to cut budget on details that we had previously and adamantly insisted on.

About two weeks before our scheduled move in, I received my new driver's license reflecting our change of address. For about twenty-four hours, I felt that we were at the finish line until the "Artful Dodger" confessed that he had spent the balance of our building funds.

Without my knowledge, he had taken those funds and reinvested into "our businesses"(one of which I did not even have entry access—I had to be buzzed in). The next day, the builder and I took a walk around the huge hole that had just been dug for the Olympic-sized swimming pool.

Speaking in a matter-of-fact manner, I said, "David, we do not have the money for closing."

He said, "Debra, what do you mean, you do not have the money for closing? This is a custom home and I have a lot of money invested in this project."

In hindsight, I'm surprised he did not push me into the hole. Once he got over the initial shock, I offered a potential solution to our problem. "Why don't you just flip our deposit from this project and sell us a less expensive house?"

He reminded me that as a custom builder he did not keep inventory. But after considering the dilemma, he reluctantly agreed to show me a house that he and his family were about to move into. Other than the fact that it was large, there was nothing about this house that appealed to me—not even the name of the street.

Standing in the foyer, I put my hands on my hips and told him, "This will do."

When I shared "Plan B" with my husband, he laughed at me and told me I could never pull it off. Ten days later we moved into the Plan B house and when we did, the builder of my dream house netted an additional $300,000 in appreciation; lucky him. I would call that a Happier Ever After moment.

I obsessed over the loss of the house and found myself driving by it at least once a week for almost a year. I would park and cry. Little did I know that life would give me something else to really cry about.

Approaching the one-year anniversary of living in the Plan B house, my husband announced he was leaving me. He had decided this while I was burying my last aunt. While I was wrangling two small children on airplanes, he was visiting condos on a golf course. While I was putting my aunt in the ground, he was breaking ground on his new bachelor pad. While my appetite waned due to grief, he was wining and dining his new love interest.

He had plotted his departure right underneath my nose. Within eleven hours of his announcement as I was unpacking from my trip, he was packing away our marriage and unpacking his boxers at his new condo.

Overnight, I was left to figure out how to raise two young children on my own while juggling a fledgling business. I had no family support at hand. His unilateral decision was heartless and calculating and consistent with his modus operandi. He said I could keep the house, along with the mortgage.

Two days after he left, I came home on a lunch break to find a house full of his warehouse workers packing up the crystal and china. But trust me when I tell you they were scattered and gone in under ten minutes.

Over time I came to understand that my *consolation* house was meant to serve has my fortress—my ark. It was not nearly as extravagant as the villa we built, but that was also a blessing because I was able to afford it on my own. It is also the house where my children grew up and affectionately referred to as home and felt safe and secure; void of tension and angst.

I can still see the smiles on their friends' faces as I served up chicken and waffles or held gingerbread house decorating contests during Christmas. If I close my eyes, I can still hear the high-pitched screams of kids playing in the distance and smell the buttery kettle corn as they huddled to watch scary movies or stayed up late to play video games.

Our home served as headquarters for my business for many years. Many clients crossed our threshold and enjoyed a steaming bowl of homemade chili or a slice of peach pie after negotiating a sizeable contract. Out of that house, my staff and I custom wrapped and shipped thousands of celebrity gifts, including the Barack Obama Christmas holiday ornaments when he was first elected.

I kept the original blueprints for the villa and my premature driver's license to remind me that things can change in an instant if they are not meant to be. God knew a storm was coming, so he sent me this house to serve as my Ark. Just like Noah used his Ark to escape disaster, my Ark "kept a roof over my head" and helped me raise two wonderful kids, sustain my business that over time became the foundation for my financial future.

Pearls of Wisdom......

Lessons Learned

1. A house is not a home. Don't get caught up in the frills of extravagance. You need a place where you can experience peace of mind, love, beauty, and happiness.
2. Anywhere you dwell should be your Queendom. Just because you don't have your dream home, even if you are in a one-bedroom apartment or efficiency, it can serve as your palace. A positive attitude, fresh flowers, and a subscription to Pinterest are a great start. If you slip into a pity party, remind yourself how many people are homeless.
3. Where there's smoke, there's fire. If a spouse will not openly discuss your financial status, there is a problem.
4. Beware of Space Invaders. If someone leaves you, always change the locks immediately.
5. Loss is relative. Obsession over something materialistic like a house pales in comparison to the death of a loved one or a marriage.
6. People don't care where you office as long as you are accessible, effective, and professional.

Current Snapshot

Stay with me on my journey to reclaim Debbie and learn how the sale of the Ark eventually funded my Happier Ever After divorce.

Who's Been Sleeping in My Bed?

Infidelity

One day I ran across a friend who was dying emotionally. I knew the signs all too well. Instead, I distractedly compared my new, awkward plumpness to her suddenly rail-thin body. After my divorce, I had developed an eating disorder, binging on food as I attempted to fill the emptiness I felt in my soul. I had previously been slender and fit, but now I was stuck with an extra fifty pounds I just couldn't seem to shed. As it turned out, my friend had the same problem as I did, just manifesting in the opposite way.

She shared with me that her husband had recently left her and their special needs child. He was a politician, manipulative and narcissistic, and she began to cry as she told me he had emotionally and financially abused her throughout their marriage. She was also a public figure and needed to be concerned with the appearance she presented to the world, so I desperately tried to calm her down through her avalanche of weeping and wailing. Her pain was so familiar. I could barely keep myself from joining in her tears. My naïve and well-meant compliment about her weight had set off a land mine in both of us.

After I got her stabilized, I left my friend, having gained a new understanding of the fragility of life and happiness. I accepted that I was being called on a mission. I knew that I had to finally lay my own pain to rest in order to help others undergoing the same process. This conversation with my friend made me realize how much there was to be gained simply from the sharing of a burden. I was soon conducting an in-depth study into the causes and effects of a failed marriage.

Before long, I came to believe that some people come into our lives only to provide a life lesson we would not learn otherwise. This was the case with my husband; for many women I spoke to, it was the case with their husbands. When you give someone ownership of your life, you allow their deceptive tendencies to redirect your path.

Deceptive people make their own broken world less painful by weaving illusions into the lives of their victims. Cunning by nature, they medicate their own disease by transferring their problems to others. How do they do it? They blame someone—anyone—else for the harmful things they say and do. They are masters of offensive strategy.

Whether their deception arises from a traumatic childhood or a long-unfulfilled desire, these people need to seek proper counseling to learn to control their compulsive behavior. Anyone who has lived with a deceptive person knows how difficult it can become to distinguish what is real from what has been fabricated on a whim. If you are on the receiving end of deception, you might begin to doubt your own sanity. Maybe you didn't really see lipstick on his collar. It could have been a bloodstain from shaving. Maybe you did sign those papers for a second mortgage on the house. You must have forgotten. His lover didn't actually call your house. It was your own insecurity fueled by your vivid imagination. What makes these situations even more difficult is that deceptive people hide their problems very effectively. Their dark secrets have a way of causing chaos in everyone's lives but their own—at least until they are caught.

If we are walking in truth, most women know when their husband has left the back door unlocked for an intruder to enter. The rhythm of the marriage feels out of sync, emotionally and physically. Tragically, when infidelity penetrates the marriage covenant, most wives fall prey to the mistake of blaming themselves: *What did I do wrong? Did I get too fat? Am I spending too much time with the children? Next she starts the game of twenty questions: Who is she? Who else knows about this? How long has this been going on? What makes her so special? Where and how often do they meet?* Far too often, her next move is to compromise herself, doubting her unique and individual worth: *I can fix this if I work out more, cut my hair, and learn to play golf. I will have sex with him more often. I will be whatever he wants me to be.*

Stop right there! Why do you have to be the problem? Don't lose your mind because your man can't keep his pants up. There is no denying that the feelings of despair, inadequacy, depression, and desperation are all real. You must address them, but this process should not start with you interrogating yourself. Cry, visit a marriage counselor, see a psychologist if necessary, but whatever you do, don't assume that you are the only catalyst for the offense.

THE SURPRISE PARTY: BRIANA
Cause of Death: Infidelity and Deception

Eric and I met in high school. His mother was my Sunday school teacher. She thought we would be a good match and introduced us when I was fifteen and he was seventeen. We dated for ten years and married once both our careers were established. He was my first lover, and, up until we divorced, my only.

When first I met him, I was impressed by the maturity and apparent stability he possessed at such a young age. His parents had divorced when he was only nine years old, and he was very devoted to his mother. Knowing this, I felt assured that I had discovered a rare gem. I had always been told that a man who has a close relationship with his mother makes a great husband. Eric's mother died while we were still dating, but when he proposed to me, he honored her by hiding my engagement ring in the music box she had long cherished.

He had a very successful career as a business consultant, which afforded us a privileged and affluent lifestyle. Since his success meant we had no need for a second income, I put my human resources career on hold until our children were older. Early in the marriage, Eric became very controlling and often seemed to ignore my presence, especially when he had an audience. He tended to blow off my opinions, but I always let it slide.

Sometimes when I came into our bedroom after making sure the children were tucked into bed, he would pretend to be asleep. I wanted to make love; he wanted to be left alone. He was pushing me away and had started to build a barrier, but I refused to acknowledge it. We had the typical marital challenges: juggling work, kids, and bills, all while trying to squeeze in time for romance. However, no other major problems or signs of impending trouble ever surfaced.

For my fortieth birthday, Eric told me he had a surprise for me. He had arranged for me to go to Chicago for a girls-only weekend. He had planned everything in meticulous detail. The highlights were VIP tickets to The Oprah Winfrey show, spa treatments at the Red Door, and, of course, shopping. I was overjoyed at his thoughtfulness and had a wonderful time over the weekend. I even saw part of Oprah's show from the famous greenroom. Using Eric's platinum American Express card, I picked up a few trinkets on Michigan Avenue. Throughout the weekend, the girls and I reflected on how lucky I was to be married to such a generous and considerate man. I was glowing!

I couldn't wait to get home and share all the details of my adventure with Eric. I returned relaxed and refreshed, but that evening, when I tried to tell him about the weekend, he seemed edgy and preoccupied. I didn't give his behavior a second thought. My tale would just have to wait until the morning. Eric had recently been traveling abroad, and I figured he was just tired. The next morning, Eric, acting very calm and collected, told me we needed to talk.

"I've made a decision," he told me. "We're getting a divorce." Just like that, after fifteen years of marriage and twenty-five years of being together, raising babies, making memories, and undergoing multiple corporate moves, our marriage was over. The incredibly thoughtful trip to Chicago was nothing more than a setup, a hoax, a bust.

I went to work in a daze that morning. Luckily, at the time I was working for a fabulous boss. After I shared the morning's news with her, she said in a very steady and knowing voice, "OK, you can cry today. Tomorrow, you start digging in drawers and making copies of everything you can get your hands on. After you get the ball rolling, I'll see you back at work, but not until you are ready."

My boss was a recent divorcée herself, and turned out to be a godsend. As she turned to leave, she added, "Do what you need to do."

After being with this man for years and watching his business dealings from afar, I knew I was headed into battle and would need all the sound advice and support I could get. I thought to myself, *Who is this man, and where is my husband? He would never do this to me, to us, to our kids.*

The man I loved was dependable and protective of those he loved. Was it was a midlife crisis? I knew such things happened. In the back of my mind, I wanted to believe that Eric had gone temporarily insane and that this situation would blow over. I prayed, but the nightmare was soon full-blown.

I tried to remain pleasant and calm, hoping I could win Eric back with my charm. I planned an appeal to his sense of reason and responsibility. I told myself I would do anything to salvage our family and to save myself and our children from the pain and humiliation of divorce.

After Eric dropped the first bomb, he told me he would stay in the house with us for a year, so he could pay off the bills; then we would get divorced. After this second announcement, he left on a campout with our son, Corey, as if nothing had happened. While they were out digging for worms, I started digging for dirt on him as my boss had instructed. I felt I had no choice, since he had clearly abandoned our marriage vows.

I checked his pockets, his desk drawers, and his briefcase. Normally, he kept his briefcase locked, but on the day I was searching it was open. He had let his guard down.

Inside the briefcase, I discovered cell phone records, bank statements, and credit card bills that might prove helpful. I found cards and letters, but the most devastating thing I found was a love note he had written to another woman on our wedding anniversary. This discovery sent me into a tailspin.

I needed to talk to someone, so I called my older brother, Winston, who told me to make copies of everything I could get my hands on and hold it all for evidence. Winston and his wife made an excuse to come and visit me; they wanted to be close in case Eric exploded when I disclosed my findings and had him served. My brother and my sister-in-law also helped me gently share the news with my mother, who surprised us by writing me a check for $10,000 to retain my very expensive attorney. "We gotta do what we gotta do," she said.

I've always believed that God reveals everything you need to know in his time. As I soon found out, Eric had been having an affair with one of his employees. His administrative assistant shared the details of what she knew with me when she learned of the rift in our household.

"Your husband has been making it impossible for me to do my job," she told me. "I can't maintain my scheduling system because he makes all these cryptic appointments. He's frequently double booked because he decides to add a meeting with a junior staff member at the last minute."

She knew I would piece together what she was not saying. I was shocked by my husband's shameless behavior, but grateful for the candid honesty of his assistant. People all around me were supportive and eager to help. My boss, knowing firsthand what I was going through, would stop by my office often and say things like, "Should I close your office door today?" or "We'll just pretend you aren't here today." My colleagues would show up at my desk with a bag from the deli because they could tell by the way my clothes hung on me that I was not eating properly.

My background in human resources really helped me through the process. To stay sane, I would compartmentalize my life's issues. When I was at work, I focused only on work. When I went home, I dealt with the children and the divorce.

When it was time to negotiate the details of the separation, I sought wise counsel. Some days I felt overwhelmed, but I would cling to something my father taught me when I was very young. "Winners never quit!" he always told me, and I didn't.

If I was particularly wound up, and needed to release my stress, I would go out to the tennis court. My game was never better than when I pretended that every tennis ball I hit was Eric's head. With the support of my family, friends, and colleagues, I was able to keep my eyes on the ultimate prize: the well-being of my children. In the end, my childhood sweetheart had turned out to be as bitter and sour as a rotten apple, but I knew the only way to taste life's sweetness again was to move forward and get on with my life.

Current Snapshot

I soon reached the understanding that my marriage to Eric was only meant for a season. Life with him had served its purpose, and had given me two wonderful children. It was not until after the divorce that I learned that I was capable of supporting my family and myself. I finally knew without question that my opinion counted and my work was valuable. Although I was initially stunned at the path my marriage had taken, it was not long before I realized that I was destined to fight my way up to a higher path.

I feel my strength now whenever I walk into a room. People tell me that my positive energy permeates my surroundings wherever I go. I am so much stronger now than I was, and I am a much better role model for my children. I was forced to come into my own after being abandoned by my husband. The road to rediscovering myself and my abilities has not been an easy one, but I can choose now not to let anything get me down.

14

Since I was so young when I met my husband, I never really dated anyone else. By dating a variety of people since my divorce, I have learned so much more about my tastes, my preferences, and myself. I am also lucky to have an amazing group of friends—especially girlfriends—who helped me through my struggles and with whom I am always happy to spend quality time. My divorce was a necessary reminder that everyone needs multiple lifelines in the form of different people who care for you. Never give up your girls for the sake of a man. Your life should always be balanced to keep both in perspective.

My faith in myself, in people, and in God survived the trauma of my divorce. I still hope I meet that special person at just the right moment, but until then I plan to have a wonderful time while I wait!

Pearls of Wisdom

From "The Surprise Party"

- Find something you look forward to doing—such as a hobby, an exercise routine, or community service—to give your life some structure and keep you going through difficult times.
- Educate yourself on the divorce process so that your spouse and his attorneys will not be able to cheat you.
- Decide what you want the end of each day to look like, and make it happen, no matter the circumstances.
- Let others help you, and focus on one issue at a time. Otherwise you will become overwhelmed.
- Live in reality. Don't ignore signs of infidelity such as emotional abuse. See things for what they really are.

- Don't get hung up on the number of years you have been with someone. If the marriage is destructive and can't be fixed, get out.

SHE WILL BE BLESSED: SHERRY
Cause of Death: Sexual Addiction

I met my husband Michael in high school. I was attracted to his winning smile, charm, and constant ability to make me laugh. We became an item after going to our senior prom together. My family did not see the potential in Michael that I did. My parents, who were divorced, agreed about little, but they were in agreement about him—and were not shy about sharing their thoughts with me. They warned me that he was sneaky and had major character flaws.

All the same, our romance blossomed over the next couple of years, and it wasn't long before we were making wedding plans. My father attended the festivities reluctantly and did not hide his displeasure in doing so. I chuckle now, on the rare occasions that I revisit my wedding album; my father had a grimace on his face. As they say, a picture is worth a thousand words!

No major issues emerged during our first few years of marriage. My life felt full and I was content. I had a husband who loved me, a family who supported me (except for my father), and good friends. I felt Michael and I had secure employment and a comfortable home, and, before long, we had an adorable baby girl. I was living my fairy tale.

Yet I began experiencing unexplainable panic attacks and horrible recurring headaches. In hindsight, these symptoms were early indicators that trouble was brewing, but at the time I thought I had more important things on my mind. My mother had stressed the importance of giving back to the community. I decided to mentor local youth. Among the teens I mentored was a sixteen-year-old girl named Arika. She was a bright girl who appeared to have academic potential, but had been victimized by the hard life of living in public housing on welfare. I asked Michael to help me mentor her. Between the two of us, we touched base with her weekly. We planned to expose her to the opportunities that a college degree or military service could offer once she graduated from high school. What I didn't know was that Arika had no intention of pursuing the options we laid before her. She thought she had found an easier way out of the projects.

It wasn't long before Arika was pregnant. Her focus shifted off the college track. I became pregnant with our second child not long after her discovery. Barely seventeen years old, Arika gave birth to an adorable baby girl she named Harlow. I rushed out and bought the things her baby would need. Periodically, I would pick up Arika and Harlow and bring them over to our house for a temporary escape from their poverty. Michael seemed irritated about their visits, and frequently asked me why I was doing so much for her. I told him that I felt we should remain supportive even though she had veered off track.

Our new baby, Jessie, was born soon after Harlow. Not long after I delivered, I had a routine checkup at my gynecologist's office. After my examination, my doctor asked if I had recently had any sexual encounters with someone other than my husband.

"Are you kidding?" I asked. "Of course not! I don't sleep around."

I was offended that he thought that I might be capable of cheating on Michael. The doctor listened to my outraged defense, then raised an eyebrow and told me that, in that case, I would need to have a difficult conversation with Michael that evening. I had contracted Chlamydia, a sexually transmitted disease. If I had not been unfaithful, it meant my husband had. My doctor looked me in the eye and asked, "Do you understand what I am saying to you?"

Of course I did; I was suffocating under the weight of the news.

When I got home, I confronted Michael immediately, passing the doctor's news on to him. Michael replied, "Who the hell have you been with, Sherry? How could you do this to us?"

But I was resolute and would not allow him to turn the tables on me. I refused to let him insult my intelligence as well as my character, and would not accept his bold-faced lies. I demanded the truth, and finally, with downcast eyes, he confessed that he had slept with his best friend Darin's wife, a woman named Rochelle. I was stunned and wondered how he could stoop so low. These were our friends! He had even been the DJ at their wedding reception.

Hurt and furious, I called Rochelle's house. Apparently Michael had tipped her off. My calls were never answered. Frustrated and tired of the games, I left an angry message on their home recorder. When I finally heard from Rochelle, the first words out of her mouth were that she was sorry. She admitted to having an affair with Michael. She made it very clear that she did not have Chlamydia or any other STD. She also said that she and Darin were going to try to work things out, and that she hoped that Michael and I could do the same.

I wasn't interested in her pep talk. I needed answers. At that point, I knew that I needed to find out how many women Michael had been sleeping with besides Rochelle. He was playing Russian roulette with my health and my life by having unprotected sex with multiple women. I confronted him again, and his answers this time blew my mind.

"Sherry, I can't tell you that I was ever faithful to you. Women are constantly approaching me, so we just . . . hook up," he told me.

When I demanded to know who these girls were and how many of them there had been, he grew evasive again.

"They're just girls," he said. "Girls from the club. Sometimes they're prostitutes. Babe, you need to know how much I love you. I will stop. I promise I will."

Suddenly, a horrible thought occurred to me as I remembered his strange behavior around Arika, the young girl we had been mentoring. "Michael, have you been with Arika? Did you father her baby?"

There was a long silence. Finally, he hung his head and admitted it.

"I am so sorry, Sherry. It just happened. I didn't know how to tell you."

So there we were. My thirty-year-old husband was Arika's get out of jail free card. He was the meal ticket and the getaway car for a mere kid determined to flee the projects. Oddly, I felt a serious sense of responsibility toward Arika.

Without a tear or a scream, I made him call her and tell her that he was coming to get her. When he brought her back to our house, I could not even muster anger toward her or her child. I asked her straightforwardly if my husband was her baby's father. Locking eyes with me, she told me he was. I closed my eyes and thought back to the time I had naively held his teenaged mistress's baby in my arms while I carried my own child, his child, in my womb. How could he do this to me, to us? How would we explain this to our children one day?

In hindsight Baby Harlow looked just like Michael. I asked her what Michael had done to help with the baby. She said he had provided only two packs of diapers. To compound an already horrible situation, Michael had lost his job the same week our second child was born. There was no way he could have been contributing to the care of her baby. He was not even contributing to our household.

My anger was directed squarely at Michael. Arika had not taken a vow before God to honor, love, and respect me. It was Michael who had made this commitment.

Arika's motives were clear to me. She saw that Michael had a car, a house, and money in the bank. She was, however, oblivious to the fact that I was a very big part of the equation, as I was the major contributor to the resources she thought she had a claim to.

I found out later that, in desperation, Michael had demanded that Arika get an abortion when he learned of her pregnancy. When she refused, he beat her up—hoping to make her lose the baby—but the pregnancy endured. Suddenly, the three of us were discussing paternity issues instead of SATs and college applications as I had once hoped. I was also busy praying that this girl would not bring charges of statutory rape against Michael.

With lots of prayer and counseling, we tried to work it out. Once the secret was out, Michael was granted legal visitation rights to see Harlow. At one point, Arika said she needed a break from childcare, so Harlow stayed with us for about two months. While she was with us, I noticed she had a hernia, so I tried to have the baby added to my insurance policy. The clerk on the phone took issue with me because I had missed the normal enrollment period to add a new baby to the policy. I explained that I was not Harlow's biological parent, that my husband had her out of wedlock, and that

I had only recently found out about her existence. As soon as these facts came to light, the clerk put her on my policy without hesitation and told me that I would be blessed for my compassion.

Once I had Harlow insured I took her to our pediatrician's office. Knowing that I had just had a baby boy, the nurse asked what our relationship was after commenting on how pretty she was. I told her the baby was my husband's. Obviously taken aback, she too told me that I would be blessed for my generous behavior, and shared that her husband had also had a child outside of their marriage.

Not long after I accepted Harlow into our life, Michael's antics became even more suspicious. He avoided the house and stayed out later and later. He misjudged me by assuming that I would go along with his behavior no matter the circumstances. One night he had the nerve to come home at 5:30 a.m. He had supposedly been at a disk jockey engagement, but I knew it should have only lasted until midnight.

That night, I knew there was nothing to salvage from this mockery of a marriage. When he stepped inside the door, I confronted him. "I don't know where you've been," I told him, "but you need to pack up and go back there. I will not deal with this craziness anymore. You have to leave, and you have to leave now."

He looked stunned, but I blazed on. "Michael, get some things. You can come back later and get the rest of your stuff."

As if in a daze, he slowly replied, "You can't do this to me. Where do you expect me to go?"

I had finally shut this circus down. "Where you should go is no longer my problem. You can start by going to hell," I said. When he left, I lay down on the couch and felt peace for the first time in long time.

We were divorced within ninety days. The marriage could not be resuscitated; the farce had gone on far too long. My mother and my girlfriends provided the support I needed to get through that difficult time. One friend was my researcher and helped me evaluate my divorce options. Another was my pragmatist and helped me keep my household running. Another was my optimist and always did her best to keep my spirits high. All of them helped with my children. With God's grace, these girls saw me through a very difficult time of my life, and I will always be grateful to them.

Current Snapshot

After the divorce, I did everything I could to return stability to our household. I thank God that he gave me the courage to walk away from Michael and never look back. The nurse I told about my husband's child out of wedlock was right. I am abundantly blessed now—better off than I would have ever been had I stayed in the marriage.

I had never had a personal relationship with God until all of this happened, but the fallout from the destruction of my marriage forced me to seek God for myself. I started going to church. I read in the Bible everything my mother and grandmother had been trying to tell me over the years.

I had never finished my undergraduate degree, but after the divorce I felt compelled to elevate myself. As soon as I completed my bachelor's degree, I jumped right back in and started work on my master's. Meanwhile, a close friend of mine reconnected me with an old friend from our high school, a man named Bruce. Our courtship was slow and steady, but his constant support of my ambitions and my children eventually won me over and we married. Not only could we laugh about old times, but he loved my children and would even help me research and edit my papers for school. I knew I had found something special, and I thank God every day for my blessings.

Late one night, several years after my divorce, a constable came to the door looking for Michael. I told him that I was no longer Michael's wife, that I had remarried, and that I did not know how to reach him. Apparently, the state had recently forced Arika to identify her baby's father or lose her welfare. It turned out that Michael had subsequently fathered twins by her, but had never met or taken responsibility for them. I left it to the judge to break this news to him.

Bruce has been my rock every day since we married. I know I can count on him, as he has seen me through more struggles than I could have envisioned when we first started dating, including my battle against breast cancer. My many attempts at caring for those Michael had left wounded in his wake finally paid off; today I have a man who cares for me, regardless of the scars I have from old wounds long ago suffered.

Pearls of Wisdom.....

From "She Will Be Blessed"

- All women—married and single—need to request regular STD screenings during their visits to the OB/GYN.
- Do not disregard signs that your marriage is in trouble. If your friends or family strongly disapprove, or you suffer from subconscious emotional outbursts such as panic attacks, heed the warning that something is amiss in your relationship.
- A man who honors you and your marriage will not engage in chronic extramarital affairs. If he does, get out of the marriage.
- Never let yesterday overshadow your tomorrow.

THE WRONG GIRL: MARVELLA
Cause of Death: Immigration Fraud

I am Officer McClinton, and I am an adjudicator for the United States Bureau of Citizenship and Immigration. For the most part, I have a happy job: I help make people's dreams come true by facilitating their citizenship and legal immigration into our great country. My job is pretty routine. I deal with forms, site visits, and personal interviews. The most crucial part of my job is to make sure no fraud transpires during the application process.

There is one particular phenomenon that occurs in my line of business, something we call *immigration love*. This phrase refers to an arranged marriage that takes place purely for the sake of an immigrant obtaining a green card. It is a pervasive issue, and very profitable for many. It is morally wrong and very illegal, but it happens all the time, and the methods for evading the authorities have become rather sophisticated. If I ever sense that a marriage or engagement is a farce, it is my duty to investigate the situation—and to nullify the administration of the green card if the relationship turns out to be a fraud. These investigations can be exhausting at times. Fortunately for me, there are some cases in which the immigrant's spouse does my work for me. Marvella was just such a woman.

One day I came into the office to process what I thought would be a regular caseload of interviews. These interviews are step two on the road to citizenship. The first step is the application process. If all goes well, a green card will be conferred to the applicant based on the sponsorship of a spouse or family member. After a minimum of two or three years, the green card holder can apply for permanent citizenship, but in order to do so, they must first pass the interview screening.

A smug-looking man from Nigeria named Swabena was first on my list this particular day. He had initially come to the country on a student visa and was currently working in information systems. His wife, Marvella, accompanied him. What struck me first about Marvella was her outfit: she wore an ensemble more formal than what I usually saw in the office. Her outfit befitted some special occasion. Her dress, shoes, and handbag all seemed to be after-five attire. Her briefcase, on the other hand, stood in direct contrast to her cocktail attire. Interviewees did not need to remit any documents, so I wondered where she could be headed with a briefcase full of documents after our meeting.

After I finished the preliminaries, I asked Marvella, "As a United States citizen in good standing, and as his wife, you are sponsoring your husband's application for a green card, correct?"

I soon found out why she brought her briefcase. Marvella rolled her eyes and shook her head as she started shuffling through some papers, then waved them over Swabena's head. "Not so fast, Kunta Kinte. I'm 'bout to ship yo' two-timing ashy butt back to the motherland, back to yo' mama, and back to that trick you just can't seem to live without!"

Barely pausing to take a breath, she continued, "You can say good-bye to the subways, the Yankees, the Giants, the Knicks, the Statue of Liberty, the hot dogs—and speaking of dogs, that's exactly what you are, you American wannabe." She turned back to me and said, "I may not have much, but I have the power to put an end to his trifling ways." She slid some papers across my desk and went on. "I am petitioning to withdraw his application. Our marriage has been a scam. He used me. He has a wife and children over in Africa."

The disgust in her voice was palpable. I looked over at Swabena. I swear I have never seen a black man turn as many shades of gray as he did then. He did not say a word, just looked as surprised as I was by Marvella's angry declaration. At that point, I asked Marvella to step out of the room with me, and took her to an area where we could talk privately.

I offered her a beverage and asked if she cared to explain herself. Did she understand what her withdrawal would mean to his citizenship process? Before I could finish, she started ranting again. She threw pictures and miscellaneous documents across the table. Her briefcase was apparently stuffed with endless evidence of Swabena's ulterior motives.

"Swabena and I met 'bout fifteen months ago at a bangin' club. That night was magical. He was the perfect gentleman, asked me to dance, bought me drinks, was better than all them moochers I was so tired of. That night I told him that I had two kids, and wasn't married to either of my babies' daddies. Even after hearing I had baby drama, he stuck around. Conversation just flowed. He told me I needed a good man in my life and a good church home. I thought I had finally found a man that didn't judge me by my past. After that, we was together all the time.

"He was all considerate, buying me little things, taking me to dinner. He even started fixing thangs up in my house. He met my kids, and they loved him from the start. After that, he said we ought'a take them on pretty much all our dates. He bought them toys and really acted like the daddy my kids ain't never had. My parents thought he was the answer to they prayers. Anyone who could get me outta the clubs, change the way I used to dress, and get me goin' ta church and my kids into Sunday school was golden to them. They was so excited when he proposed even though we was only been dating for two months. To me, it just felt right.

"My momma and I started planning my dream wedding, which included all of my girls as bridesmaids. I was the first of my group to finally walk down the aisle. They all told me they was glad to see me so happy. It made them believe it just a matter of time before they Prince Charming found them."

She pulled photos from the wedding out of her briefcase to show me. "After the wedding, we signed the marriage license an' his application for a green card. Swabena said it was easier to handle all the legal stuff at the same time, and that made sense to me. I wanted my man to be rockin' the red, white, and blue ASAP.

One day I was on his computer and saw some trick's name that I ain't recognize pop up on his Facebook page. I ain't nosy, but I thought that, I'm his woman, I gots a right to read the message. It said, "I miss you, when is this going to be over?"

"I started sweatin' an' napped up the press and curl I just paid fifty dollars for. I wanted to put him on blast to my parents, but I decided that for once I would keep my big mouth shut. My momma would have told me to look the other way, since I finally got a good man willin' to take care of me an' my kids. Instead, I told my girls, who said I better find out what that African was really up to. They knew right away that something wasn't right.

"After that meeting, I was checking his e-mail and Facebook page whenever I could. One night after he fell asleep I found an email that he sent this ho. It read, I miss you too, baby, and this marriage has only been a means to an end. The first thing we're going to do once we get you over to America is have a real marriage, and make you a citizen just like me. I sent some more money, give some to my mother.

"I told myself he ain't going to use me no more. I called my girls to help me do the research, and we figured out how to take the rhythm out of his bongos and block his green card . . . So no, Officer McClinton, I ain't sponsoring nothin'.

He's got the wrong girl, and you can mail his drum-beatin', two-timin' ass right back to his woman in the straw hut. But before you do, you can give him this for me." With that, she reached back into her briefcase and flung a thick envelope across the table. I opened it up and found a petition for divorce inside.

As far as I was concerned, the interview with her was over. I told her, "Miss, you are a United States citizen in good standing and have no further business with the Department of Immigration. There is no need to detain you further. I am so sorry this happened to you. You are free to go, and good luck with the rest of your life."

Marvella got up and strutted out of the office. Her girls were standing right outside the door and started cheering as soon as she made her triumphant exit. They gave each other high fives and hugs all the way out the door. As I headed back to the interview room, everyone in the office was talking about our latest immigration love bust. By then, my supervisor was interrogating Swabena and explaining the consequences of his attempt to defraud the United States of America. My coworker Clarissa rushed up to me with a huge grin on her face and asked, "Did you get her phone number? I know those girls are going to be partying tonight, and I want to be wherever they are!"

Current Snapshot

Although it would be against protocol for me to keep in touch with Marvella, I have every reason to believe she is doing just fine. It took a lot of courage to do what she did. She faced the obvious—that she was being used by a man whose only intention was to gain citizenship in the US— and stood up for herself, her interests, and her well-being.

Plenty of women would have turned the other cheek, just as her mother might have suggested, for the sake of financial assistance or the false sense of security that having a man around the house would suggest. Marvella was not interested in compromises, though. She knew she deserved better and was not afraid to go after it.

Pearls of Wisdom......

From "The Wrong Girl"

- Do not rush into a marriage, especially when you are dealing with a foreigner who is not a legal citizen. Do your homework: investigate their background, and, above all, be sure they are trustworthy and love you for who you are, not for your legal status.
- Don't pour your heart out to strangers. There are too many predators out there like Swabena who will prey on your weaknesses to gain your trust and confidence.
- Be careful when exposing your young children to new people. Children are both impressionable and vulnerable.
- Don't allow your spouse to isolate you from your friends. If he attempts to, take this as a warning that he fears one of them may be on to him about a less savory aspect of his intentions toward you.

THERE'S NO PLACE LIKE HOME: RACHAEL
Cause of Death: Infidelity

When I found the playful satin boxers he had not received from me and had never worn for me, I felt like someone had punched me in the stomach. The discovery set me off on a witch hunt. The tiny pieces of shredded paper I found at the bottom of his trash can screamed at my internal radar. I intuitively knew that the author didn't want the words on them to be read ever again. With the precision of a sleuth and the determination of a crazed maniac, I taped more than eighty pieces of paper together and read what my heart already knew. I pieced together his pathetic plea as my world fell apart; just like a lovesick schoolboy, he begged my secretary to love him.

I had not scheduled a nervous breakdown for that day, so I raced to my office in an attempt to settle my nerves, wishing I had never attempted to validate my suspicions. After a while, one of my many employees came into my office. In the middle of our discussion about a routine business matter, I turned the meeting into a heaving, wailing snot fest. As it became increasingly obvious that I would not be able to compose myself, I sneaked out the back door so my other employees would not see me falling apart. I despised the majority of them for their vicious and idle gossip.

As I slipped away to my car, I called home and instructed our housekeeper to pack three bags: one for me, one for my infant daughter, Taylor, and one for my young son, Max. I didn't know where we were going at that point, but I knew my world was caving in, and I was running away from my fraudulent marriage and everything that made me want to die.

When I got home, I called a close friend to tell her that I was having a moment. She told me she was about to drive to Atlanta with her two sons to see her folks. Recently divorced herself, she understood my dilemma. We had developed a silent language. She offered to take my son along with her. My little guy was glad to be headed on an exciting adventure with "Auntie Katie" and his best buds. Little did he know that his mother was broken down, depressed, and empty. I was unraveling at the seams and desperately in need of a break from life as I knew it. Once I had

Max on his merry little way, I had my executive assistant make travel arrangements for Taylor and me. We were going to the only place I knew was safe: home.

After we landed, I jumped in a cab as if I was a tourist and made the long journey to the big, red brick house. Thirty minutes later, I stood trembling on my daddy's porch. When he answered the door, I shoved the baby into his arms and nearly collapsed. No words needed to be exchanged. He knew. He had always known, but had kept his thoughts to himself all these years. My sister heard the commotion and came downstairs to greet us.

As much as I needed my mother right then, I thanked God that she was not alive because it would have killed her all over again to see her once-rambunctious daughter in this condition. I asked my sister if she would take care of Taylor for a couple of days and take me to the train station. Plane, taxi, train—by the time I lay my head down that night, I had taken them all. I was on a mission to escape all the noise in my mind and find peace.

My sanity awaited me in San Diego, where my son's godmother had assembled her family to celebrate her mother's birthday. I was going to show up to be built up. I was always welcome wherever they were. I cried all the way down the coast. I didn't care who saw me. These faceless and nameless people on the train didn't know or care that I was running from life. In San Diego, the beach would refresh my soul. I needed the waves to carry me back to myself.

I envisioned walking the beach, my hair flying in the wind, relieved of my business suit, deadlines, and fake smiles. I was going to let the fresh air fill my lungs so that I could breathe again. I was going to rest my brain so that I could think again. Above all, I was going to surround myself with genuine love and lots of laughter so that I could smile again.

Two days on the beach, late-night walks along the shore, and earnest talks with my friend Pilar rejuvenated me. I felt strong enough to trek back to the only home I had ever known, to the fortress where, no matter what, I would be met with my daddy's twinkling eyes and strong, loving arms ready to protect me from the rest of the world.

When she was alive, my mother used to tell me that what happens in the dark always comes out in the light. Her wisdom rang true in my marriage. When I returned to my life in Des Moines, my thinking was keen, and I was able to start objectively evaluating the broken pieces of my marriage.

It turned out that my husband had been paying off the housekeeper and other employees so that they would keep their mouths shut about his extracurricular activities. I found sorrow and relief in the same last breath. My marriage and my father died within months of each other, and when they did it was as if time stood still. I didn't deal well with either death; I reacted by throwing myself into my work. Rarely did I sleep or eat. When I went to bed at night, I was so exhausted I didn't have the energy to grieve; I just collapsed.

Current Snapshot

I can't tell you the day it happened, but one day I knew I was going to be OK. Life was finally good again. I got there with a lot of prayer and self encouragement. My mother died when I was very young, so I don't have many tangible memories of her, like photos or video. Luckily I have several home videos of my dad. When I'm lonely and need to feel a paternal presence, I pop one of the videos of him into the DVD player and wrap myself up in his humor and love. I have the feeling that my parents are in heaven right now petitioning God to send me the man that was created especially for me. I pray that I will never be married to someone who does not value me or my sincere commitment to marriage. As for my ex-husband— him I do not miss. Some people and circumstances are better left in the past. If only in my mind, my parents' big red brick house will always be my home and refuge, a place of unconditional love and acceptance.

Pearls of Wisdom....

From "There's No Place Like Home"

- If you feel extremely saddened and stressed, take some downtime by any means necessary, before you have a nervous breakdown or sink into a debilitating depression.
- Children feed off their parents' energy—both good and bad. Be careful of exposing them to your mood swings.
- Make sure you always have a safe place to go or a trusted person to whom you can turn.
- Always keep emergency money or a credit card with available funds. You never know when you might have to make a mad dash for sanity's sake.
- No one can ever steal the love you have for a person or place that dwells in your heart.

CORONER'S REPORT ON INFIDELITY

PHYLLIS J. GEE M.D. F.A.C.O.G of Health Central Women's Care P.A. and owner of Willowbend Health & Wellness Associates

In over twenty-five years of private practice, I have encountered numerous female patients who have spent their lives supporting their husbands' careers, raising their children, and putting their own needs to the side—only to find out that their husband is cheating. These selfless women are taken off guard, left to figure out how to rebuild a life for themselves and by themselves, very often without the financial resources or career options to do so. This is enough to put anyone in a state of panic. In these situations, the first thing these women need to do is take stock of their own emotional and physical health.

As the potential first responder to a woman's plea for help after she discovers infidelity in her marriage, the gynecologic community has the excellent opportunity to engage in a real, candid discussion about a woman's overall physical and emotional health and well-being in the wake of this occurrence.

Screening for STDs is an essential first step. In this day and age, no one can afford to keep their head in the sand when it comes to such a serious matter. We offer numerous referrals and resources to women who find themselves in this painful situation. On occasion, I have sadly been the one to break the news to patients who presented with nonspecific symptoms during a routine exam and then tested positive for a sexually transmitted disease. These women leave my office distraught and go home to have a difficult discussion with their spouse.

The medical community needs to do a better job of educating women about the benefits of STD screening even if they believe they are in a monogamous relationship. Ladies, you need to be in charge of your health just as you are in charge of your checkbook. If your health care provider does not ask you if you want to be tested periodically for STDs, then you should request it. Remember that if you are being emotionally or physically abused, it is quite possible that your partner is also unfaithful.

High levels of stress resulting from the demise of a marriage can lead to numerous other ailments and disorders in women, including excessive weight gain or loss, heart palpitations, mood changes, depression, and insomnia. Many of these symptoms relate not only to the direct effect of stress on the body, but have a lot to do with the emotional response to stress itself. A woman's mind-set has much to do with how well she can cope with trying circumstances. I need to underscore here that stress can kill. Heart disease is the number one cause of death in women.

We cannot ignore the role that our psyche plays in our body's dance with disease. When I learn that a patient is experiencing divorce, I encourage her to take extra steps in self-care. There is no "magic pill" to cure a broken heart. However, being aware of your mental and physical state is key when it comes to combating the catastrophic illnesses that can be triggered by an inordinate amount of stress from a life-changing occurrence like divorce.

Stress Reduction:

- Identify your greatest sources of stress and eliminate them as best you can.
- Minimize your contact with people who contribute more stress than joy to your life.
- Exercise regularly and get plenty of sleep.
- Learn to laugh.
- Learn to love yourself first.
- Avoid overexertion and schedule leisure activities away from your routine work.
- Build meditation, relaxation, or prayer into your life to serve your emotional needs.
- Promote your mind-body connection.
- Equally important in combating stress is a healthy, non-toxic diet.

Health Enhancement:

- Stick to a diet that is well balanced, rich in whole foods (such as fresh fruits and vegetables and whole grains), high in fiber (at least twenty-five grams per day), rich in good fats (such as omega 3, polyunsaturated, and monounsaturated), and sufficient in lean protein and low-fat organic dairy.
- Limit salt, alcohol, caffeine, fried foods, and partially hydrogenated and saturated fats.
- Avoid refined carbohydrates, trans-fatty acids, and nicotine.
- Eat a good breakfast and don't skip meals.
- Drink plenty of water daily.
- Consider participating in a whole-food detoxification program at least once a year.

Nutritional supplements are still necessary to sustain your good health, and they will help to restore key nutrients depleted during periods of stress. Supplement a healthy diet with whole-food multivitamins, antioxidants, and vitamin B complex. Finally, seek counsel and treatment from a trusted health-care provider for specific complaints. Seeking the counsel of a licensed psychologist, therapist, or marriage counselor is key to promoting the mind-body connection. The medical community can offer numerous referrals and resources to women who find themselves in this painful situation.

You have only one life to live. Fill your prescription for life by making a daily commitment to honor your body, manage your stress, and foster your mind-body connection— especially if you have the misfortune of experiencing a divorce.

TRACY D. SHAW, PHD, Licensed Clinical Psychologist and Relationship Expert, on the Importance of Self-Esteem

For many women, infidelity is the match that ignites a destructive fire in a marriage. Infidelity can rapidly destroy an otherwise viable family. This significant betrayal of trust often creates an immediate feeling of powerlessness and helplessness. Unlike some of the other culprits that attack the marital covenant, such as substance addictions or physical abuse, this is the one area in which too many women automatically assume they have done something to cause the situation. Far too many women blame themselves for the adulterous affairs of their husbands. As a licensed psychologist, I have witnessed firsthand how infidelity and its side effects (e.g., verbal, emotional, and psychological abuse) can destroy the self-confidence of women.

What is self-confidence? Self-confidence is how you view yourself. Self-confidence depends on how strongly you believe in yourself and your abilities. Self-confidence allows you to take risks in your life. Self-confidence is at the heart of every soul. Without self-confidence, a woman doubts her worth. Without self-confidence, a woman begins to question her beliefs, her intelligence, and her feelings. In the face of infidelity, a once self-assured and determined woman can start down the path of emotional and psychological neglect, all thanks to the destruction of her happily-ever-after fairy tale.

Let's examine the emotional, psychological, and interpersonal devastation that infidelity can bring about:

Emotional Impact

- Rage
- Disbelief
- Crying spells
- Discouragement

- Sadness
- Anger
- Mood swings
- Frustration
- Irritability
- Psychological impact
- Difficulty concentrating
- Forgetfulness
- Poor motivation
- Low productivity
- Negative attitude
- Confusion
- Lethargy
- Boredom
- Negative self-talk

Impact on Relationships

- Isolation
- Intolerance
- Resentment
- Loneliness
- Lashing out
- Mistrust
- Alienation

It is unnecessary for women to suffer in silence from the emotional and psychological consequences of infidelity. There are many steps a woman can take in order to rebuild self-confidence and avoid self-destruction.

Building Self-Esteem

1. Cultivate your inner voice:

Do you ever hear what you're saying to yourself? Sometimes women act as their own worst abuser by putting themselves down or constantly criticizing themselves. Take the step to replace your negative dialogue with yourself with positive and self-affirming thoughts.

2. **Face your challenges with strength and determination:** Learn how to confront—rather than avoid—the challenges you face. Our life is a powerful weapon if we empower ourselves not only to speak the truth but to live a life of truth, facing reality as it is. Acknowledge your accomplishments, no matter how insignificant they may seem to you. Recognizing the challenges you have overcome allows you to begin to understand your gifts and talents. Infidelity may or may not lead to the death of your marriage, but it can certainly provide you with the opportunity to reexamine your strengths and priorities.

3. **Uncover your assertiveness:** Remind yourself that you have a voice that deserves to be heard. Take hold of the ability to exercise your personal rights. Learn to be assertive, and practice clear, honest communication. Give yourself permission to share your opinion and your beliefs. Say what you mean, and be clear on what you do and do not want.

4. **Nurture mindfulness in your life:** Pay attention to your emotions and don't be afraid of them. Don't allow yourself to waste away in a false reality. Empower yourself to manage your emotions effectively by setting healthy and appropriate boundaries. Choose to be wise and choose to be strong.

These simple tips can illuminate the pathway of success for those who are faced with most women's nightmare—infidelity. Women must open their eyes to the emotional and psychological development that awaits them when trust is broken and a marriage has checked in to intensive care. Women cannot allow themselves to waste away in denial. Self-development is our own responsibility, and it is the empowerment we require to fulfill our God-given purpose.

ELDER CATHY MOFFITT, Founder and President of Heartfelt International Ministries, on Living Through Adultery

Infidelity wove its way through the fabric of my own family and caused us much grief and pain over the years. It also taught me how important it is for everyone affected by these situations to witness and participate in the forgiveness process. Because of my firsthand experience, I vowed to God that these lessons would be paramount in my teachings when I was called to the ministry to coach and mentor women.

Adultery is a decision between two people that interrupts the lives of all those who are close to them. It destroys reputations, causes hurt, and casts lasting negative repercussions on the lives of all involved.

Some women respond to uncovering their husband's adultery by trying to outwardly improve themselves, losing weight, or changing their wardrobe. This is a superficial response to a deeper underlying problem, and it pains me to see women lowering themselves to beg for love. When all else fails, some women even commit the same act of adultery as their husbands. They seek retribution by trying to cause their husbands to suffer as they have, and in doing so perpetuate the suffering of all.

The Word of God is clear on this subject. It reads, ". . . to avoid fornication, let every man have his own wife, and let every woman have her own husband" (1 Corinthians 7:2). The devil will try to convince you that you can escape the consequences of your actions—but trust me, you can't. Neither can we stop sin in our lives on our own. We can only do so with the help of Christ, through true repentance and total forgiveness. Adultery is a sin; this much is clear. Just as with all other sins, we must go to God for healing and deliverance.

Whatever choices you have made or pain you have experienced, trust in the forgiving power of the Lord Jesus Christ. If your husband cheated on you and broke your heart, take your broken heart to God. If you cheated on your husband or with someone else's husband, take your cheating self to God. You will find there is always enough room for you at the cross. After you have given your burdens to God, know that you will be stronger, wiser, better, and renewed for experiencing the test of infidelity.

> *Dear heavenly Father,*
> *I pray now for each woman who has been victimized by or participated in adultery. Please allow your Holy Spirit to comfort, heal, and deliver her, and reveal your glory in her life. Offer her forgiveness as you teach her to forgive and seek forgiveness. Offer her peace when her heart is broken with despair. Offer her your cross and teach her that after suffering there will be victory. In the name of Jesus, I pray.*

Unroyal Treatment

Physical Abuse

Domestic violence does not discriminate. It is no respecter of poverty or wealth, of ethnicity or religion. Shelters are filled with women who fled beautifully decorated homes that were filled with violence and shattered lives. Those who are bold enough to flee are often the lucky ones. They sought refuge and lived to tell their stories.

One out of every four women I interviewed for this book admitted to having experienced some form of domestic violence or assault during the disintegration of her marriage. On average, a woman will not leave an abusive situation until the seventh assault. Once I understood the frequency and severity, I started regularly visiting the criminal courts in order to listen to cases firsthand. On one of these field trips I even heard the case of a woman who was murdered by her husband and brother-in-law. Unlike what you see on TV, there were no bright lights or scripted lines—this was domestic violence reality on steroids. I learned that many women of affluence go to great lengths to keep their cases out of the courts because they do not want to jeopardize their lifestyle or become the hot topic at the country club.

The city of Grapevine, Texas—an affluent suburb of Dallas—made national news when an estranged husband showed up on Christmas morning disguised in a Santa Claus suit and opened fire on his wife and five other family members. A total of seven people were dead by the time his rampage burned itself out. When the tragedy hit the news wires, the locals were shocked that such a thing could take place in their safe, sheltered enclave.

Far too many women have been subjected to acts of domestic violence, and far too many women keep these travesties a secret. No woman should allow her body to be brutalized. No woman should accept her suffering as the result of her own poor choice in a mate. There is nothing a woman can say to a man that can excuse his hitting her. No child should have to witness their mother being beat down like an animal. People who brutalize others are monsters, but we can only stop them if we refuse to continue sweeping the issue under the rug. Your life is worth more than your possessions. There are plenty of resources available to help battered women, but they can only help you if you are willing to let them.

I know one woman who finally decided she had had enough of being kicked and slapped around. One night, she loaded what she could pack in her car, grabbed her young daughter, and moved into a new apartment. They had no furniture, nothing but a mattress to sit on. She gave up everything to take charge of her life, and she is such an inspiration to me. When she left her former husband she did more than just save herself; she saved her young daughter from mimicking a victim mentality. If her story inspires anyone else to leave an abusive situation, then she has helped save them too.

If you have been pushed, choked, shoved, slapped, kicked, punched, bitten, or spat upon, the time has come for a change. Take all threats seriously. If a man tells you he is going to harm you—or worse yet, kill you—believe him. The following chapter contains the stories of women who mustered the willpower to say enough and remove themselves from harm's way. I hope they will inspire you to put your life in perspective if you are being bullied or physically assaulted.

In a Heartbeat: Diana
Cause of Death: Physical, Emotional, and Substance Abuse

Dennis and I met because we lived in the same apartment building. We had immediate chemistry and a mutual physical attraction. We dated for a couple of years and then decided to get married. What I had not realized at the time was that he was an alcoholic, as I had seen no signs of it during our courtship.

About five years into the marriage, when our daughter was still an infant, he became increasingly aggressive. He would punch holes in the wall when he was angry. We got into shouting matches, and before long, he started hitting me instead of the walls. The first time he hit me, I hit him back. I couldn't believe what had happened, but I was not going to let him think that I couldn't protect myself. I had never been a pushover, and I was determined not to become one now.

But then Dennis started doing drugs and the fights escalated. I backed down when the beatings became routine. He was much stronger than I was, and I knew I couldn't keep up with him. I was also afraid of what might happen to our daughter if Dennis didn't stay focused on me.

I was from a large family and had two brothers and many male cousins. If any of them had known that Dennis was beating me, they would have killed him before asking further questions. But I never said a word to any of them. I was afraid of the outcome, and I didn't want to be responsible for any more violence. Instead, I focused on hiding my bruises and scars until I could escape. One time Dennis slapped my face so hard that my eyes bled on the inside. I considered myself lucky that I did not lose my eyesight. To cover up the bruising, I wore sunglasses for three weeks straight—as if they were nothing more than my latest fashion accessory.

Initially, I stuck with the marriage because I thought that things would change. I convinced myself that I needed to keep trying to love him, for our daughter's sake, and hold on to hope that he would get better. I did not want to face the fact that I had exercised poor judgment in selecting a life mate. I dealt with my problems by pouring myself into my work, and my work became my escape.

I ran a well-respected business and was responsible for the tour scheduling of nationally recognized recording artists, actors, and playwrights, but the truth was that I couldn't handle my own business at home. I was a battered woman, and I was too afraid and ashamed to ask for help. On the outside, I appeared vibrant, happy, and successful. On the inside, I was dead and numb, and I felt like an imposter of myself.

Dennis and I stayed together for another ten years while I preserved my facade and tried to protect him from himself, doing everything I could to keep him away from jail and out of harm's way. I especially did not want our daughter, Tiffany, to see her father's dark side, but I knew in my gut that she had witnessed my beatings. Her knowledge was made obvious by her behavior. She became more and more quiet and withdrawn. She always looked sad and scared, but I could see her trying to appear to be happy and strong for me.

I could no longer deny that Tiffany deserved better. No child should have to live in such a volatile home environment. I had thought that I was the only one acting through the pain, but Tiffany had already started to follow my lead by the time she was ten years old. I knew something would have to change, because the last thing I wanted was for my daughter to continue following in my footsteps. Still, I was petrified. This life had become my normal, and I didn't know how to escape it.

Late one night, Dennis came home drunk out of his mind. He accused me of having an affair, which, of course, I wasn't. He threw me to the floor, pinned me down, and kept punching me until I almost blacked out. I was just conscious enough to summon up the words to the Lord's Prayer. Over and over, I repeated the phrase, "and deliver us from evil." The power of the words finally seemed to get to him, and he got up off me.

I never did get a chance to plan my escape. About six months after that episode, he burst into my bedroom one morning before dawn. He was foaming at the mouth like a rabid dog and his eyes were glazed over. He was holding a large pot of boiling water and told me he was going to "mess me up."

It was clear to me then that the man had lost his mind, and intended to do irreparable damage to me. I did not have the skill, training, or desire to calm him down. I will never be certain how I got out of the bedroom that day, but I know God had a hand in it. As soon as I slipped away from him, I screamed frantically for Tiffany and told her to run to the car as quickly as she could. We both fled early that morning with nothing but the pajamas we wore.

As we sped out of the garage, I focused on only one thing: escaping with our lives intact. I had no plan and no thought for where we could go, but somehow I found myself driving to a colleague's house. It was as if my car had gotten us there on autopilot. Finally, I took off my mask and admitted to her that I had been in an abusive relationship for years.

I realized that my silence had almost cost me my life. I had no emotions left and could not even summon up the strength to feel embarrassment. Later that morning, I borrowed clothes for the two of us to wear and took Tiffany to school. Then my adrenaline kicked in. I went to the courthouse to file a restraining order. The police followed me home and forced him to leave. I had finally made the first crucial step in freeing myself and my child from this sick man.

I still had to run the business and worked between ten and twelve hours a day. If I hadn't had Tiffany to take care of, I probably would never have left the office. The friend who took us in on the day of our escape helped with the business and with my daughter. In spite of the chaos of my personal life, I was razor-sharp at work, and the business soared. I funneled my newfound energy into building the business and stockpiling money for Tiffany's future.

I spent the next seven years battling my ex-husband over money and assets, 90 percent of which were rightfully mine. With his drug addiction, Dennis couldn't keep a job and was determined to get half of what I had broken my back to build while he was snorting and smoking anything he could get his hands on. But I was determined not to let him rob me. I wanted to be able to support my daughter in the lifestyle that we both deserved.

The stress of life and struggle to separate from Dennis took its toll on me, but I kept pushing. Friends and family begged me to quit haggling over "stuff" and just finalize the divorce. As much as I wanted to move on with my life, I was determined to win this fight. I worked like a fiend, and eventually the stress caught up with me.

During the Christmas holidays, some friends insisted I stop by their holiday party. I only stayed a short while because I suddenly felt exhausted. When I went home and got in bed, I couldn't get comfortable. My chest felt oddly tight. The pain increased, and once again I found myself screaming for Tiffany. She took one look at me and called 911.

The paramedics arrived, and, after some quick tests, rushed me to the hospital. Luckily, it was just around the corner. Later, the doctors told me that if I had arrived five minutes later, I would have died that night. I had suffered a massive heart attack, and doctors determined that I had more than 85 percent blockage in all four major arteries. A few days later, I was being prepped for a quadruple bypass. I was barely forty-five years old at the time.

This was the catalyst I needed to finally close the chapter on Dennis in the book of my life. I had denied myself happiness for too long, first by staying with him, then by continuing to battle him for the sake of principle and material things. I realized that, had I died on the operating table, none of those things would have mattered, and my daughter would have been left in the care of an addict. When we went to the final hearing for our divorce, I prevailed in all of my requests, but by then I was prepared to compromise if necessary just to get on with my life. After I completed my final testimonial, the judge told Dennis, "I don't know what kind of offer she has made you, but I suggest that you take it."

Current Snapshot

After the divorce, my daughter confessed that she had known about the beatings, but had always been afraid to tell me. Amazingly, she is well adjusted now, and seems to have fully recovered from the ordeal. We have a wonderful relationship, and she tells me I had every right to leave her daddy. Today, that is all the confirmation I need to hear.

Throughout the nine years of our separation, Dennis never paid a dime in child support. As the saying goes, however, "Every dog will have his day." Dennis finally stepped up to the plate to support Tiffany while she attends college, and she is doing well at school. For me, the journey of raising her is over, and I have no need for his money today.

I am now living in my dream house with all new furnishings and driving my dream car, a convertible Lexus. I have met my soul mate. He is a wonderful man who has established a successful entertainment business. Finally I have a man who doesn't need rescuing. Instead, he prides himself on making me happy. What more could a girl ask for?

My health is now great as well. It turned out that my heart attack stemmed from the high blood pressure I had inherited from my parents. The almost-invisible battle scar that runs down the center of my chest is my badge of courage. I don't try to hide it; it reminds me each day to cherish the precious gift of life and to count my blessings while I have them.

Pearls of Wisdom......

From "In a Heartbeat"

- The first time someone hits you, walk away. Don't let it happen a second time. There is no reason to risk endangering your life. Do not tolerate physical abuse under any circumstances.

- Seek out counseling and support when things get bad.
- If you pursue a divorce, hire a competent attorney but stay as involved as you can in the proceedings. No one knows as well as you what you want the outcome to be.
- Protect your children from drama. Your problems should not become theirs. If they witness any of the violence, talk to them about it and seek counseling for them.
- Don't risk your life or livelihood trying to help a spouse who is an addict. There will always be a point at which you need to draw the line and save yourself.

Setting the Record Straight: Marla
Cause of Death: Sexual, Physical, and Emotional Abuse

From the day I was conceived, I was doomed by my mother's demons. She used men and Jack Daniels to make life tolerable. I was born from that darkness and became the target of her rage. I was not born to live, and I never knew what it was like to be loved or valued. When I was young, I only ever felt the emptiness that came from being ignored and abused in every imaginable way.

I was the sixth child in a set of children my mother had conceived with multiple men. Eventually, she married a man named David and had three more children with him. Still a child myself, I became the resident babysitter. I also became the object of my stepfather's unbridled sexual whims when my mother was too drunk to perform her "wifely duties." By the time I was eight, he had repeatedly molested me—often with my younger sister sleeping soundly in the same bed. I was bound by shame and silenced by the fear he had instilled in me. Whenever I tried to tell my mother what David had done to me, she turned a deaf ear. To acknowledge the truth would have obligated her to leave David, and she made it abundantly clear which of us she valued more.

At this stage in my life, I had no idea who my real father was. At the age of fifteen, when I couldn't take living with my mother and David any longer, I ran away from home—right into the arms of more abusers. I was taken in by a couple who was acquainted with one of my older half-sisters. Gerald and Janet said they would protect me, and I wanted so badly to believe them that I convinced myself it was true.

But it wasn't long before Gerald started molesting me. I was terrified of what would happen if Janet discovered that I had been with her husband. One night, she rushed into the bathroom behind me as I walked through the door and locked the two of us in. I was certain she was going to kill me then and there. I closed my eyes and prepared for the worst.

Instead, she gently touched my face and proceeded to unbutton my blouse. It had never dawned on me that a woman could molest me too. The more she fondled me, the more confused I became. *Why would she do this?* I wondered. At one point, I remember thinking, *At least she isn't beating me.* I knew I wasn't supposed to like what was she was doing, but, after a while, I allowed myself to be overcome by her sensual touch. Her touch was soft and loving, unlike any man I'd ever known. She was the first person I had ever known who seemed to value me, and I was carried away.

Almost immediately, I embraced a lesbian lifestyle. I felt powerful and in control for the first time in my life. I found confidence in the thought that, if I played the role of a man (as I was being groomed to do), I could control my situation and never be a victim again. With another woman, I finally found the love and validation my mother had never given me.

But all that time I failed to see that these impulses came from the deep wounds left by my mother's disinterest in me.

These wounds had never healed and continued to control my thoughts and behavior. When my mother suddenly came close to dying, I made a pact with God that I would get my life on track if he would only save her.

He did, and so I kept my promise even though I struggled immensely. I left my hometown in order to escape my past. Before long, still hoping to elude my demons, I married, but the marriage was destined to fail from the beginning. My husband was newly widowed and acted out his grief on me. I rationalized the situation, telling myself that at least I had kept my commitment to God. I did not immediately tell my husband about my own past because I was so embarrassed and ashamed.

Riddled with guilt, one night I finally confessed to him how my life had evolved out of chaos and repeated molestations. I thought he would understand why I had done what I did. I hoped that he would comfort me. He did neither. Instead, he beat his anger into me. But I was finished with letting people act out their rage and disappointment on me.

I kept my word to myself that I would never be victimized again and divorced him soon after the attack. I was proud that I had taken control, but I was on the run again. It would be many years before I managed to forge for myself a life that was worth living, but at least I had finally taken the first step in the right direction.

Current Snapshot

I eventually found healing and self-worth through writing, the theatre, and the church. I met and married my current husband, Erik. From the beginning, our relationship was founded on laughter, mutual respect, and honesty. Erik has taught me that you have no option but to be yourself, even when someone is trying to change you.

I love my relationship with my husband because I feel that it is what God intended for me all along. We have both become ministers and constantly live in truth. I am honest about my past even when it is difficult, because I have seen how my honesty can liberate others. I lived a long time in darkness and deceit, and I know just how damaging a secret life can be.

The rage that once pulsed beneath my skin is gone. Somehow, in spite of the trauma of my early life, God preserved my capacity to love. Finally, I feel alive because I feel God's unconditional love and the love of God through my husband. I spent the early parts of my life in a desperate search to be validated. My liberation only came when I freed myself by forgiving all of my abusers, starting with my mother.

I made peace with my mother before she died. I have since published more than a dozen books. My business is thriving, and my husband and I co-pastor a church. Our ministry emphasizes healing battered and emotionally compromised women and men. When Erik first told me that he loved me in spite of my past, I knew that at last I had been blessed with authentic love. I know I am blessed to have found someone who loves me in spite of the darkness I came from. If I can overcome such demons as I have, I know that others can do the same, and I hope my story encourages other women like me to battle their way toward the light.

Pearls of Wisdom......

From "Setting the Record Straight"

- No matter what terrible things have happened to you in the past, you must take responsibility for your future and strive to make wise decisions.

- The only way to embrace love fully is through openness and honesty.
- There is no shame in true love, for true love casts out all fear and shame.

HURRICANE JEFF: DANIELLE
Cause of Death: Physical Abuse, Infidelity, Suicide

Jeff and I had barely been married for four months and were still paying off wedding expenses. When I told Jeff we could not afford to buy his nephew a bike for Christmas, his immediate response was to fling me across the room like a ragdoll. I was in no way intending to be selfish or trying to emasculate him. I was merely being honest. We were struggling to support the six children we had between the two of us. I worked as a correctional officer after Hurricane Katrina; I was the only one with a job for a while. My paycheck was not enough to keep us afloat so we struggled.

Within a week of the beating over the bike, my husband knocked me down a flight of stairs. When I hit the ground, I blacked out and had to get sixteen stitches. This was only the beginning. Before the battering had started, he had been so kind and attentive, and helpful with my children. After the first few incidents, I weighed my alternatives and decided to stay put. I constantly tried not to provoke him. When he went into one of his rages, I would fight back if I could muster up the strength.

I also suspected that he was being unfaithful, but I had my hands too full to play the sleuth. I didn't want to invite the unthinkable into our already complex marriage, but my suspicions were confirmed when I discovered that he had recently fathered a baby by another woman. When he became aggressive with my children, I packed up and moved to a friend's—but he followed me. He stalked me day in and day out and even at my place of work. He would call me and if he got someone else, he demanded to talk to me. Not only did this behavior frighten me, it also jeopardized my livelihood.

One night, he showed up at my job and sat in the dark parking lot in his black car waiting for me to come out. I didn't see him. After he slipped up on me, he punched me in the face. Luckily, my supervisor saw me on her way outside to be an onlooker to a fatal incident that had just occurred on the freeway. She attempted to come to my aid, but with his aggressiveness, he didn't too much allow her to help. I gave Jeff his ring back on the spot, and told him I couldn't keep trying. I moved out immediately and began the process of filing for divorce.

He wouldn't let me take anything substantial with me when I left, so right before the next school term started, I went back to the house to gather more of my children's belongings. After I left the house, he jumped into my car and locked the door, saying that he needed talk to me. I headed toward the nearby Walmart, thinking that a four-block ride would be harmless. Those four blocks were the longest ride of my life.

En route, I received a phone call informing me that two of my coworkers had died. The news upset me particularly because I had just talked to and seen them not that long ago. When I stopped the car in the Walmart parking lot, Jeff was trying to reconcile with me. He didn't care that I had just received startling news. As I started to get out of the car, he grabbed my hand, "I just have one more question," he said. "Can we work things out?" My answer was the same as it had been before. "No!" I said.

In one fluid motion, he pulled out a gun, put it to my head as I turned to get out of the car, and shot me. I staggered out of the car, unable to process what had happened. When I started to feel a vibrating sensation in my head, I shouted somebody please help me and a lady shouted, somebody give me a cell phone, she's been shot. My next words were "Lord, please help me." I put my finger to my temple and felt the blood running down my face.

She rushed to my side. I begged her not to leave me, but she noticed there had been movement in the car. She apparently thought there could be a child in danger and approached the passenger's window as I lay bleeding. When she got to the window, she discovered my husband. She told me later that she heard Jeff say, "My wife is gone. I can't live in this world without my wife." He turned the gun on himself. My husband succeeded in his suicide, but not in my murder.

As I was preparing to go through some of my first emergency surgeries, I signed the papers to release his body to his family so that they could bury him in our native Louisiana. Not only did I release his physical body that day, I released him and all that he represented. He was buried on the same day that I had the first of my eight reconstructive surgeries. I spent the next five months enduring seemingly endless operations and treatments to repair a broken bone behind my right eye, a shattered retina, a cracked skull, the pierced lining to my brain, the mangled bones in my nose, and my shattered jaw. The fact that I lived at all remains a miracle, but I knew all along that I had to move forward from the horror in order to raise my children. I took tremendous comfort from the knowledge that I would never again have to deal with Jeff's raging storms.

Current Snapshot

I can't say that I am happy that Jeff died, but I am so grateful that I am alive today. People ask me all the time if I have forgiven him for what he did to me, but the answer is easy for me. What's not to forgive? I don't wish hell on anyone. If I held a grudge, I would create hell on earth for myself, and I will not allow him the satisfaction. No one forgets the kind of thing I experienced, but I refuse to let it run my life. I only hope that he had the chance to make peace with God before he took his last breath.

Everyone deserves a second chance to get life right. I am so grateful that I got mine. I never question why this happened to me and I never will. God is my counselor and my rock, and I believe that I went through the shooting so that I could be transformed and empowered to save other people. I am a new creature now. I am more patient, spiritual, and grounded. My prayer was answered the moment I said, "Lord, help me!"

I am a sheriff now, and I take my job very seriously. My new husband is a sheriff as well. When it comes to domestic violence cases, we are both extremely committed to helping the victims. He is spiritually grounded and has helped me in my faith. He has also made my children his children (legally), and we are eagerly awaiting our tripletts that are on the way!

Pearls of Wisdom.....

From "Hurricane Jeff"

- If you must reenter the space of an abuser, never go alone. It is preferable to have law-enforcement officials accompany you.
- When you stay in an abusive situation, you are sending a message to your assailant that the behavior is acceptable.
- Love has a better chance of lasting when you grow into it.

- Never let anyone force their way into your car or obligate/ mandate themselves in your life without your consent.
- First and foremost, remember to put and keep God first in your life at all times. With God nothing is impossible! We can do all things through Christ, who strengthens us.

Coroner's Report on Physical Abuse

Theresa Little, **Licensed Social Worker and Advocate for Survivors of Domestic Violence**

As our case studies demonstrate, physical abuse is no respecter of education, occupation, ethnicity, or affluence. If you are in an abusive situation, you can get out if you want to. Your escape will require you to put pride aside and put fear in its proper perspective. Reach out and grab the hand of an advocate—someone who knows the path to safety, just like a conductor on the Underground Railroad.

If you find yourself in an abusive relationship, do not try to rationalize the behavior of your attacker or believe for a moment that it was ever your fault. Plan your escape and get out as quickly as possible. Just like a yellow traffic sign, the early warnings of domestic violence indicate that grave danger is ahead. Proceed with caution, and understand that eventually domestic violence will lead to death.

Even if the attack begins verbally and then escalates to become physical, a batterer is a batterer. The bottom line is that a batterer isolates and mistreats his victims. In the case of emotional abuse, the attacker goes after the victim's self-confidence, with the intention of making her feel bad enough about herself until she is disconnected from her own feelings and the outside world.

If you are being physically abused, at some point it is very likely that you will have to flee at a moment's notice to save your own life. The first thing you should do is to go somewhere you cannot be found by your abuser, even if that means resorting to a shelter. If you go somewhere familiar, you are more likely to be found, and an assailant will make it his business to stalk and find you.

Escaping to a shelter does not mean you are homeless or that you do not have the capacity to earn your own wages. Fleeing to a shelter signifies that you understand the gravity of your situation. God did not create you to be a punching bag. All shelters have the same general objective—to stop domestic violence through intervention.

Many incredible success stories are told of women who have emerged stronger and more self-sufficient as a result of a stay in a shelter. Some have gone on to start businesses, earn college degrees, and become leaders in their communities. The beauty of their stories is that many return to help and empower others in similar circumstances. These survivors have taken their tests and turned them into testimonies. I have personally counseled and been inspired by countless women who have triumphed over an abusive situation and emerged stronger and more empowered. Whether they fled to an empty apartment or sought refuge at a shelter, their courage to leave all the "stuff" we think we can't live without is life-changing.

The Safe Campus concept is simple. They provide everything women and children need to stay safe and escape from their batterers at one confidential location. Services include intensive counseling, medical care, psychological evaluation, daycare and after-school programs for children, as well as job, technical, and life skills training for adults, all easily and safely accessible.

If you have not yet had to run, take all threats seriously. If a man tells you he is going to kill you, believe him. Don't try to rationalize or make excuses for him; leave that job to the professionals.

If you have been in a chronic physically abusive situation, it is prudent to have a get-away bag (GAB) packed and hidden just in case you have to run for your life. Here's what to pack in the get-away bag:

- Proof of identification (a copy of your driver's license, Social Security card, passport, visa, marriage license/ divorce decree, birth certificate for you and any dependents)
- Insurance policies (medical, life, etc.)
- Prescription medications
- Mementos (just a few to connect you to the positive part of your past)
- Emergency change of clothing for each person fleeing with you
- Gold jewelry or precious stones (these can be liquidated for emergency funds)
- If you have children, a special toy for each
- Cash

Where should you keep the bag? Not at your house or car trunk. Keep it at an undisclosed, safe place or with someone you can absolutely trust—and hope you never need it.

INSIGHTS ON DOMESTIC VIOLENCE VICTIMS, Told by Arresting Police Officers

Overt signs of a physically abused woman:

"She will not make eye contact. She is typically soft-spoken and cautious with her words. She is almost invisible. Her emotion is gone; nothing fazes her. This woman thinks she has nothing. She forgets what is his is half hers. She has buried her own leverage, her power to escape theoretical death. He bullies her into thinking she has no rights and makes it his business to keep her ignorant, scared, and in the dark. Many women who are tied to material possessions are selling themselves out, no differently than a hooker would. But a woman's dignity should never be for sale."

Dying for a honeymoon:

"My beat is in a very affluent neighborhood; the average house size is 5,000–8,000 square feet. The only people who would believe the large amounts of bizarre domestic calls that I respond to would be my colleagues. Sadly, more and more domestic violence cases are very habitual, predictable, and cyclical. First there is the anger, aggression, emotional and/or physical abuse, then the brief honeymoon period where the couple is in love again and the make-up sex is intense. The patterned behavior of physical abuse is understood by both abuser and victim; too often its occurrence also becomes routine. It's a dangerous dance that countless women don't survive because they don't get out when they can."

Protecting the monster:

"I have taken women to the shelter and—before I could finish up my paperwork at the court—they have packed up and gone back home. I remember one woman in particular whose head was gashed wide open from her husband repeatedly beating her with a metal Tonka toy truck. I stopped counting the number of stitches they had to put in her head. I guess she felt more comfortable with the monster she lived with than facing the uncertainty and possibilities of the future—which could have been bright."

Stay-at-home moms are an increasing target of domestic violence:

"A trend on the rise is the number of stay-at-home moms who are emotional wrecks and victims of domestic violence. The husband lures her into financial dependency. That leaves her with little to no option. With that in mind, he takes extreme steps to keep her suppressed, insecure, and terrorized. He counts on the fact that these women are used to maintaining a certain lifestyle. This makes it difficult for her to leave. So she hunkers down and bears the emotional and physical pain. Too often, she is willing to risk her life in exchange for the keys to a Mercedes or for the privilege of clinging to a Coach handbag filled with credit cards.

"Many husbands who are celebrities, corporate executives, community leaders, and even ministers have friends in influential places who will collaborate with him, cover his story, and, if need be, help him tie up all the financial resources in hopes of making her back down. It happens all the time.

"Then comes the final blow: he threatens to take the children if she ever tries to leave him. He knows that the children are her lifeline. He knows that she will do anything to hang on to her children. He will gamble that the courts will side with him because she does not have comparable financial resources to take care of them. He leverages this to keep her where he wants her—right underneath his thumb. The man will maliciously take the children, knowing that it will crush his wife because the children have become her universe.

"Just to add salt to the wound, he will make his children his young mistress's special project. Most times, this intruder could care less about the welfare of the children. As long as she is getting her goodies, she will go along with the charade.

Confused and manipulated, these poor kids become the ultimate pawn in a very dangerous game of chess. These children sometimes act out their pain by displaying negative behavior. In extreme cases, I've seen some of these broken children from once-stable homes become a part of the criminal system."

"Then there's the point of no return. Feeling they have nothing to lose, the man will threaten to kill his estranged or recently divorced wife. If a man threatens to kill you, believe him. Do not stay around to try to figure out if he is bluffing. Call the police, and let us do our job."

CARLA BEAN, Assistant District Attorney, Domestic Violence Division, on the Mislabeling of Domestic Violence

A core problem in addressing the domestic violence epidemic is the refusal to describe the behavior for what it is: a conscious choice to use violence or threats to get a desired result. Although the law specifically defines what physical or verbal acts constitute domestic or family violence, there is a widespread unwillingness to accept the straightforward definition. This breeds distortion and encourages deception. Mislabeling is a common practice because it is more comfortable to describe the slap, punch, or threat to kill as a "marital conflict" or a "relationship issue" rather than labeling it domestic violence.

In one case I encountered, a woman who was a 911 operator and trained to use accurate terminology still selected the term "restrained" rather than "strangled" when describing how she lost consciousness during her assault. Similarly, an abuser who paraded around the living room with a raised ax in hand insisted that no "family violence" had occurred because he never put his hands on his wife.

Mislabeling is a dangerous practice, particularly when the abuser is the one with the ax.

Simply put, abusers choose to do what they do, and their choice affects everyone in the family. Abusers choose to brutalize partners by burning them with hot irons, choose to kick pregnant wives in the stomach, choose to point a loaded gun in the face of their mate, or choose to terrorize someone by stalking them. It is important to realize that the abuser's choice to be violent impacts more people than just the immediate victim. There is pervasive emotional hurt and psychological harm to other family members, including children, grandchildren, nieces, nephews, and siblings. Children who witness such violence often imitate it as youngsters or duplicate it as adults.

The abuser's choice to be violent often causes family members to choose sides, forcing them to align themselves with either the abuser or the victim. Siblings may cease communicating; family members may testify for or against either party. Such division can cause intense hostility, anger, and resentment—especially when the violence is disclosed after many years of abuse. A case in point involved a marriage where physical and verbal abuse began in the first year and continued until the couple's separation some fifty years later. After a seventy-three-year-old wife reported the physical assault by her seventy-six-year-old husband, she was applauded for doing so by one child and discouraged from calling the police by the other. Reaction to the horrific photos of this woman's injuries also varied among her family members, ranging from disbelief to anger at the victim for exposing the family secret.

Fear of exposure plays a major role in how well the criminal justice system accommodates the parties in domestic violence cases. The fear of being exposed is the abuser's greatest fear, while the fear of being identified may be the victim's. Many women choose not to seek out safety tools such as protective orders due to their fear that neighbors, coworkers, or family members will learn of their secret life as the victim of domestic violence. Unmasking an abusive situation may seem risky, but exposing the abuser's true identity by reporting abuse or seeking protective orders can be a powerful tool for regaining control.

The Wizard of Fraud

Financial Abuse

Money cannot buy love or happiness. It is important not to lose sight of this fact of life. However, I don't think that anyone will argue the fact that money is required for survival in this world. You cannot keep a roof over your head, nourish your body, drive a car, or provide for your children's health and well-being without it. When money is mismanaged or falls into the hands of the wrong person, it can destroy lives. When someone steals your money, they make you a victim. Falsifying your financial records or forcing you to enter into loan agreements against your will is an act of abuse, and as such deserves to be treated seriously. Not only does financial abuse hurt immensely, it undermines the victim's independence and strips away her dignity and self-reliance. Financial abuse has been known to derail brilliant careers, bankrupt self-esteem, and leave the victim powerless to defend herself.

Intimidation and emotional manipulation are usually at play in situations of financial abuse. The attacker might say things like, "If you love me, then you'll cosign for my car loan," "I need you to ask your parents to lend me money for my business venture," "You need to make me the beneficiary of your insurance policies," "I need to have signing authority on all your company bank accounts," or even "Now that your parents are dead, here's how we should spend your inheritance." The more skillful the abuser is, the more thoroughly he will convince you that his financial manipulations are your idea, or that what's best for him is best for you as well. Far too often, however, the woman who walks ignorantly into this trap ends up committing financial suicide.

When I asked victims of financial abuse what it felt like to be robbed of their assets and left to pay bills that they didn't create, here are some of the responses I received:

> "I felt paralyzed by my own inability to keep up with my bills."
>
> "I was always stressed. I didn't know how I was going to make it, and I was angry at myself for ignoring the obvious. I thought I should have known better—I have a law degree!"
>
> "I should have turned him in to the authorities when I could. What he did to me was a crime; he should have served time like any other criminal. But I didn't want my children to have to visit their father in prison, so I didn't prosecute."
>
> "I feel stupid for making myself so vulnerable. Anyone who would do this to his wife could never have been in love with her."

"I didn't want to lose my marriage over money issues, but now I've lost my handle on both my relationship and my finances. The next time someone asks me to marry them, there will be a prenuptial agreement—or there will be no wedding."

If you have children and are knowingly a victim of financial abuse, then doing nothing about it makes you an accomplice to the crime. You are jeopardizing not only your own financial future and emotional security, but theirs as well. If you are being coerced to do something financially uncomfortable to you, or if you discover that your credit score is being compromised, take appropriate action immediately. You will suffer the consequences, and possibly never fully recover from the trauma. Financial rapists do not linger with their victims. They move on, leaving your life in ruin behind them. Get ahead of their deadly game before it destroys you. Financial abuse is just like any other heinous offense. It merits prosecution, but that move is up to you.

DEADBEAT DONALD: HARRIETT
Cause of Death: Financial and Emotional Dysfunction, Chronic Liar

When my sister introduced me to Donald that warm spring evening, she thought she was doing me a favor. She knew I was lonely and wanted a man in my life. She also knew that, since my divorce four years earlier, the only men I seemed to meet were already married. She thought she could give my love life a jump-start by introducing me to a man who was single, attractive, and well employed. My sister was already acquainted with his niece, so she felt that it would be easy for us to investigate his past if the need arose.

The relationship's greatest draw for me was the spiritual connection we seemed to share. Our courtship started as a long-distance one. I lived in New Jersey, and Donald lived in Virginia and worked in Washington, DC for a transportation company. In the first four months, we spent an enormous amount of time on the phone. We spoke four to five times a day and often talked long into the late hours of the night. I was overjoyed to finally have a person in my life who made so much time for me.

As autumn rolled around, he said he wanted to move closer to me. He told me he hated not being with me all the time. I asked him how he planned to relocate, since he didn't have a job lined up in New Jersey. He readily volunteered to commute. Since his current job offered him free transportation, he suggested that he move in with me and commute back to DC until he could find a job in the area. I was reluctant, but I rationalized that since my youngest child, Josh, had just gone to live with his father and my oldest child was away at college, there was no real risk in letting Donald move in with me.

When Donald moved to New Jersey, he asked if he could contribute less than half of the household budget because he was behind on some bills, and had to pay child support for three children. I told him absolutely not. "If you want to move in with me, you need to contribute your fair share," I told him. "I have no desire to support a man." He said that he understood, and that he would work things out.

When he first moved in, his company took the sting out of my empty nest. Since it was just the two of us alone in the house, I felt confident that we would have some time to get to know each other without the responsibility of children to distract us. We had been living together for a year when we started making plans to get married.

Just a few days before our wedding, a woman from his past somehow got my home phone number and called to warn me that I was "getting in bed with the devil." She said that Donald was a deadbeat and that he would only use me the way he had used her. She said that he had conned her into cosigning for a car, and then left her to deal with the mess after he defaulted on his payments.

This phone call should have been my first warning sign, but instead I dismissed her as a jealous, bitter woman. I told her to lose my number and never to call me again, and continued with my wedding plans. All five of our children participated in the ceremony. Together, Donald and I decided that Josh should live with us after the wedding. Josh seemed to look up to Donald, and we thought that we could provide a positive environment for my son. I secretly hoped having an estimable male role model in the house would diminish the grudge Josh held against me for divorcing his father and accelerate his healing. All three of Donald's children were minors and continued living with their mother.

Donald had reserved a beautiful, luxurious room at a local hotel for our wedding night. When we arrived at the check-in desk, the clerk informed us that Donald's credit card would not cover the room. My new husband rambled on about how he had the money, but must have overused his card getting his kids ready for our wedding. I paid for the room, fuming at first, but soon convinced myself to calm down. Donald and I had just committed to spending a lifetime together, so I thought I should do my best to get past this ordeal and show some understanding. My sense of calm, however, was short-lived.

The original plan had been for us to continue on to Atlantic City for a week. When Donald told me that he did not have enough cash to pay for the rest of the honeymoon, I was furious and asked him exactly how much he was able to cover. He told me he only had enough for one night, so one night was the total sum of our honeymoon.

Next we deposited all of our monetary wedding presents (most of which came from my family and friends) into a joint household account. Donald insisted that we open the account at his bank since they already knew him there. Within sixty days of our opening the account, one of our mortgage payments bounced. I had owned my home for more than five years and had previously experienced no problems, so I was quite surprised when the bank called and asked me if there was a problem that they needed to know about. This was merely a courtesy call, the banker said, because I had been such a good client up until now. I was unable to fit the pieces of the puzzle together, because I had written the check to cover the payment not long ago and had a copy of the check in my register.

The next morning I dropped by the bank to get some answers and inform someone about the obvious error. I demanded that they pull out the records, and soon discovered that Donald had linked his personal account to our new joint household account. The banker told me the only way I could detach the accounts and put an end to his fraudulent behavior was to get his approval. I was stunned. Why hadn't the bank demanded that he get my signature before he jeopardized my credit?

When he walked through the door that evening, I confronted him. He said that he had "borrowed" from our joint account because his ex-wife had pressured him to catch up on his child support. He also claimed he would soon pay it back. I told him that he was jeopardizing the roof over my children's head and that I couldn't stand for it. He begged my forgiveness, and things settled down on the surface—but now my radar was up.

One day, I decided to stay home from work to do a little detective work on Donald's finances. I went through his personal paperwork to see if any more surprises were on the horizon and found a letter from his bank disinviting him from doing business with them anymore. He had bounced twenty-six checks in less than a year.

Meanwhile, Donald had shown up back at the house. "Baby, could you come outside for a minute?" Donald said excitedly. "Look! I've been at the car dealer, and I want you to check out this great 4x4 I want to buy."

The dealer who was with him said, "Don't you love it? All we need is your signature to finalize the paperwork!"

"Why do you need my signature when I'm not purchasing a car?" I asked.

"You've got great credit!" the dealer said, as if that explained matters. "You could get anything you want!"

"How did you get access to my credit report?" I asked, looking over at Donald.

Sheepishly, he whispered, "Baby, I gave him your Social Security number so he could check your credit rating."

That was enough for me. "Big boys pay for their own toys," I told them as I turned around and walked back into the house. When Donald came inside, I asked him where he planned to get the down payment for the car. As it turned out, not only had he planned to qualify for the loan based on my credit, he had also planned to trade in the car I had given him back when the one his brother had given him died. This man was a professional freeloader.

At that point, our relationship took a fatal nosedive. He started lecturing me about how we should work together more as a couple. "When one of us hurts," he said forcefully, "the other one should hurt."

I started to wonder if he was out of his mind. Then he said, "Babe, I know we can work through this and come out on top."

We? I thought. *How did I get myself hitched to a sponge?*

Donald broke into my private thoughts again, interjecting, "Oh, by the way, I've got IRS problems. It would help me a lot if you would allow us to joint file our taxes."

At this point, I was seriously wondering if I had married an optimistic lunatic. For the sake of my own sanity, I knew I had to identify all the potential land mines. In my mind, I traced back through everything he had ever said or done that raised a question mark in my head. The one thing that kept bubbling to the top was the mysterious little pill he took every day. Before we were married, Donald told me that he had bad sinuses, and he took a pill every day to keep them in check. Now, I wondered about the truth of this explanation. I went through the drawers in his dresser and turned up a bottle labeled "Zoloft." It sounded like something I had seen on TV commercials, but I didn't recall it being for sinus ailments. I called my sister, who happened to be a doctor, to express my concerns. She explained what the pills were to me, saying that Donald was probably battling chronic depression.

That same night, Donald and I got into another financially charged argument. This time it was over my life insurance policy. He asked again whether I had changed it to make him the primary beneficiary. To get him off my back, I told him that I would make the change soon, but that he needed to take a chill pill. He still knew nothing about my little pharmaceutical discovery, but the phrase "chill pill" set him off. He grew angry and started shaking my chair so hard that I had to hold onto the kitchen table to keep from falling.

I had previously scheduled a routine surgery in the upcoming week. That night, I thought, *Call the divorce attorney as soon as you are home and settled after the surgery, and see how quickly you can get him out of here.* A few days later, I went in for what was supposed to be laparoscopic hysterectomy. Things did not go smoothly, and my children told me later that Donald had rushed home excitedly from the hospital to tell them that it was "touch-and-go." He apparently thought or hoped that I was going to die and believed I had already changed the insurance policy. When I got home from the hospital and learned about his selfish performance, I asked him to leave. I had a stomach full of stitches that hurt like hell, and I couldn't stand the thought of being in the house with him for another day. I needed some peace to recuperate and get on with my life. I told myself that the charade was over and it was time to face the truth: I had married a total deadbeat, and one with a mental disturbance to boot.

About two weeks after he left my house, he took up with a woman from our church. They would frequently walk into church arm in arm. She would strut like a proud peacock, thinking she had caught a good man. Seeing them together initially hurt my feelings, and the church gossips had a field day. My consolation, however, lay in the fact that I knew the truth about him. Thanks to my sister's support and encouragement, I got through this very embarrassing time.

Current Snapshot

The day of our final divorce proceeding, Donald told me that he did not want a divorce after all. He said that we had so much in common and that he felt we could still make it. I wondered how many times he had practiced those lines in the mirror. Since the divorce, I have never once looked back, and I thank God that he delivered me from a potentially very bad situation.

I got out of the marriage before Donald could ruin my credit. In court, I was awarded a judgment against him that he has yet to pay me. Nonetheless, I own a lovely three-level home and have ample money to pay my bills, travel when I feel like it, and maintain a sizeable savings account. I am grateful each day that I was given a second chance and that I escaped from Donald before he could make things any worse for me.

Pearls of Wisdom......

From "Deadbeat Donald"

- Are you planning to marry? Get your fiancé's Social Security number and obtain his credit report. Are there any negatives?
- Beware of a man who does not have his own home and transportation. This is a red flag and warns of financial dependence.
- Loneliness has its own distinct scent. When you are lonely, you are far more likely to compromise your standards. Men who can sense this about you will take advantage of it, and you are particularly susceptible to being their prey if you have not acknowledged the issue to yourself.
- Women need to take time to heal as they move from one relationship to another. Women are nurturers by nature. Far too often, after they have been left alone, they will jump into a new project without a second thought— especially if the project is a man who seems both needy and humble. Be very, very careful to whom you open up your heart.

On a Moment's Notice: Darla
Cause of Death: Financial Mismanagement

Before I married Clarke, I had triple-A credit and a very cushy bank account. Shortly before we married, I decided to buy a new car. Within twenty minutes at the credit union, they told me to just go out and pick whatever I wanted. I selected a sleek BMW and was proud of the fact that I, unlike so many other women, had no need for a man to buy me the things I required or desired. I was fully able to finance my own whims.

I had always been conservative with my spending and saved for rainy days, but my financial modus operandi changed after I married Clarke. Suddenly it seemed as if the sky was continually raining unforeseen bills. We were constantly in the midst of financial chaos and discord, always plugging holes in a leaky ship. Of course, he never took responsibility for the problems and never used his financial resources to plug the holes. Flamboyant and extravagant, he lived above his own means and my dwindling resources.

Not long into the marriage, I started finding entries in his check register, along with cancelled checks, each in excess of $5,000. Deep down, I knew then that something was very wrong, but I buried my doubt instead of following my intuition. It wouldn't be long before I regretted that decision.

I had credit cards with very high limits, but I made sure I always had enough money to retire my debts on a moment's notice. This didn't last long after I married. One day, Clarke told me we had to have $35,000 for his business by the end of the day or things were going to explode. He made an art of playing hot potato with his finances and had gotten into the habit of throwing them over to me to catch. He counted on the fact that I would avoid conflict at all costs. Mistakenly, I figured that if I could save the day he would see me as indispensable.

I went to the bank with tears in my eyes and a large lump in my throat, pulled out three credit cards, and instructed my banking officer to give me the cash. Instead of robbing the bank, I was robbing myself. Knowing how much I hated debt, my officer looked at me as though I had lost my mind. She leaned toward me over the table and asked in a discreet whisper if I was OK. I nodded weakly and told her I appreciated her concern. I pleaded for her to bring the forms quickly, hoping we could be done before I had the chance to change my mind. I wanted nothing more than to get this embarrassing and painful process behind me.

I had whipped out my lethal plastic as if the cards were nothing more than Monopoly money. The liability for a $35,000 cash advance rested squarely on my shoulders: the cards were in my name and attached to my credit score. Reluctantly, the officer reviewed the forms, went into the vault, and came back with a large stack of cash.

As I walked out of the bank that day, I felt as if everyone around me was staring at the idiot with the fake smile and the noose around her neck. I had entered the bank hoping to play the hero, but I left feeling like a bandit.

To this day, I cannot tell you how Clarke spent that money. I can tell you it was never spent on me. When the bills were due, I asked him if he would pay off my credit cards so I could protect my credit score. Instead, he gave me a verbal lashing that made me back down and retreat into my corner. His financial offenses only worsened after that. He emptied our personal savings from our joint bank account. Once he fell behind in his Mercedes payments by three months and his car was towed away from his office for nonpayment while he was in a meeting. When he discovered his car was gone, he called me in a panic asking for the $3,800 he needed in order to reclaim his vehicle. I think this was the only time

I ever heard him cry. He had an important meeting with a foreign dignitary that night and insisted that he had to pick him up from the hotel in style. I bailed him out again, and again received a verbal beating when I asked him to repay the funds he had borrowed from me.

His financial irresponsibility seemed to be never-ending. He would charge thousands of dollars in purchases to my personally guaranteed American Express card and run up tabs at the country club that I somehow always wound up paying. Once he built up enough back-up funds and capital, he left me. I was all alone holding a bag full of his debt.

He even controlled the divorce proceedings, because by then I had convinced myself that I did not have the emotional strength to stand up to him and seek the justice I was owed. At the time, I believed that I did not have access to the funds that would ensure me a legal defense to challenge his deceitfulness and manipulation. I now know that I could have retained legal counsel that would have annihilated him, if only I had just pointed them in the right direction and given them the green light.

By the time we finally divorced, my emergency stash was depleted and my credit was ruined. Throughout our marriage, he had tapped into all my finances like they were a community chest, and I did nothing to stop him. My story is a tragedy that never should have occurred.

Current Snapshot

I have worked very hard to teach my children the importance of being financially responsible and protecting their credit. I believe that if a man really loves you, he will not expect you to jeopardize your credit to fund his pipe dreams. If a man really loves you, he will want you to be financially secure in case of his untimely death. If I ever remarry, I will insist on a prenuptial agreement outlining the individual assets and debts we bring into the marriage.

I have struggled for years to rebuild my credit. It has been a very slow and painful process. I have finally learned that my value does not rely on how many bills I foot. I stand up for myself today because I learned the hard way what can happen when you allow someone else to take advantage of your assets.

Pearls of Wisdom.....

From "On a Moment's Notice"

- You are not an ATM machine. Do not let someone take liberties with your personal credit, even if you are married. This is especially true when you bring substantial assets into a marriage.
- Do not allow your husband to bully you into taking out a loan for which he cannot qualify on his own.
- Before you marry, exchange credit reports with your fiancé. Disclose your financial situations to each other, and discuss how you will handle future financial matters.
- Use credit cards only for true emergencies, not to finance a lifestyle.

BEATING THE ODDS: PAM
Cause of Death: Stealing from Wife's Family

Even though my father and uncle were raised poor on a farm in Mississippi, they were both smart enough to build sizeable estates in excess of millions of dollars. They were not afraid of hard work and earned an honest living as blue-collar workers after they were discharged from the military. Neither of them was impressed by material things. They amassed their assets by living frugally and following the simple motto "Always keep a dollar in your pocket."

Contrary to my family's values, my husband, Cody, was extremely materialistic and constantly moved from one financial dilemma to the next. His ego knew no limits, and his overblown professional reputation required that he maintain an extravagant lifestyle. He had ambitious entrepreneurial goals and had given the outside world the impression he had the juice to back it up. He leveraged other people's money and was always on the go, chasing down the next big business idea like an addict on the hunt for his next fix.

On rare occasions Cody would travel home to be with me and the children for the holidays. When he was around, he always seemed restless and bored. Initially he spent little time getting to know my family. However, once he figured out they were wealthy, he got busy developing his act.

Finally, Cody asked me to approach them for a sizeable loan. I refused and told him not to bother them either. They were elderly and in no position to gamble with their nest egg. I would have had no trouble asking them for a loan for just cause, such as college, graduate school, or a down payment for a house, but I had never crossed that line. I had been raised to be independent and self-sufficient. I was furious that my husband wanted to borrow from my family, and I demanded to know what was so important.

He claimed that he had a great investment opportunity for them. They stood to make a 15 percent return on their investment, he said, which was more than double what banks were paying at the time. I tried to stand my ground with him, but he cornered them in the end. They knew I did not condone this behavior, but somehow I think they were hoping that the loan would benefit me and the children indirectly. They lent Cody $125,000. I have no idea what he did with the money, and am sure they never knew what it was really for either.

Cody promised to pay them back within six months. Of course he didn't. This put tremendous pressure on me. I walked a tightrope, the fear of being exiled by my family on one side, the fear of being left by my husband on the other. I was too embarrassed to go home for the holidays. I knew that everyone wanted to ask me what had happened to the money. Aware that my marriage was strained, my father was sensitive and did not press me. All he would ask me was if I was OK. I would nod yes, but I could tell that he knew this was one of the few times in my life that I lied to him.

Finally, I told both my family and my husband that I couldn't live this way any longer. If my husband defaulted on the loan, I swore to spend the rest of my life paying back the debt, even if I had to work three jobs to do it.

I meant what I said. When I told my husband how hard it had been for me to look them in the eye knowing that he owed them money, he spewed out a lecture about how he had given them a "fantastic opportunity." Yeah, right! Begrudgingly, he finally paid them off, and I thought I could exhale at last and travel home guilt free.

It wasn't until later that I discovered he bypassed me on a second round and conned them out of an additional $90,000. I believed my husband thought he would beat the odds—that my father and uncle would die before he was forced to pay them back. They were both over eighty years old, and he was right on target. As my father lay in a coma during his final days, my uncle cornered me in the waiting room outside of the intensive care unit. He wanted to know when I thought my husband would pay back the money he owed my family. Cody divorced me right before my father died and left me with a very heavy burden I didn't create.

I am still not sure how Cody justified flying out to my father's funeral. My family was outraged by his presence, especially my uncle. We had to restrain him from jumping out of the limousine when he saw Cody. If my uncle, a large man with military training from World War II, had gotten his hands on Cody, my kids would have been burying their father and grandfather on the same day. My family was further devastated when my uncle died soon thereafter. Though he never said it, I am sure Cody was relieved. Both my father and uncle went to their graves despising him for mistreating me and using them. I wish I had had the foresight and courage to borrow from my father first. If I had, I could have hired both a psychiatrist and an aggressive divorce attorney, and avoided the disaster that hounded my father until his death.

Current Snapshot

Since then, my ex-husband has had access to significant sums of money and could have easily repaid my family's estate several times over. This would be the right and honorable thing to do, but he continues to behave as if he did nothing wrong. The way he treated my family was unethical and will probably come back to haunt him one day. You cannot blatantly swindle people and not expect to receive some retribution.

I have multiple family members who should have inherited a portion of my uncle's estate, but Cody cheated us all. In my heart of hearts, I still hope that one day he will face his demons and repay all the people that he robbed using my connection to them.

Pearls of Wisdom.....

From "Beating the Odds"

- Protect your family above all. Do not allow your spouse to borrow from your family, period. Remember that your family is not obligated to lend you or your spouse money.
- If any loans are made, make sure a legal document is signed to enforce the boundaries of the transaction.
- If your spouse refuses to repay a loan, encourage your kinfolk to take legal action. If your relatives die before repayment is made, sue on behalf of their estate.
- If your spouse becomes estranged from your family or close friends because they deny his request to borrow money, see him for the opportunist he is and cut him loose.

THE GRAND SLAM: NITA
Cause of Death: Financial Intimidation

Even though my family was upper-middle class, we lived frugally. They taught me to pay my bills on time, spend only within my means, and always have something put away for emergencies. My dad's favorite words of wisdom included "Your word is your bond" and "Understand the difference between your needs and your wants."

As a teenager, I was aware that my parents sometimes had financial challenges, but they always believed in paying their debts on time, even if it required us to cut back on some or all of our wants. As I grew up, I adopted their sensible spending philosophy. As a single woman, I spent wisely and always paid my bills as soon as I received them.

I became a corporate executive, but over time I also started a small business on the side with an initial investment of just $500. At first, this business was just a hobby. Following in my father's footsteps, I developed multiple revenue streams— just in case corporate America decided to hand me one of their notorious pink slips. My side business soon became very lucrative. When my corporate department restructured and I suddenly found myself in a job for which I had to travel over 40 percent of the time, I resigned with confidence, knowing I could convert my hobby into a sustainable and profitable business.

Then my husband arrived on the scene. Preston was a successful corporate executive with lofty financial dreams. As brilliant as he was, his flaws lay in his arrogance and his tendency to color outside the lines, usually with other people's crayons. I think he thought of himself as being a kindred spirit to Donald Trump, but he lacked the cash, conscience, and practical understanding to back up his lofty ambitions. He never took debts seriously and paid bills with whatever was left after he fed his fancies.

The bigger the financial hole he dug, the more I would scramble to fill it with any resources I could get my hands on. As I did so, I failed to acknowledge that I was digging a deeper ditch for myself. I couldn't stand the thought of creditors tracking me down at work or home, so I tried to silence them with my personal funds.

Preston and I were a tragic combination, and our continuous financial drama soon became a very dangerous dance. I was petrified of losing everything I had worked so hard to achieve, especially my credit. I was also afraid of not living up to the morals my parents had ingrained in me. At the same time, I was terrified of being left alone if I did not help my husband achieve his entrepreneurial dreams.

I was pregnant when we took out our first business loan for $50,000 at his insistence. He said that we needed the money "for capital improvements." He said that I was too conservative in my approach to business, and that I was sabotaging my company's unlimited potential. He was relentless. Not wanting to argue about business at home or jeopardize my pregnancy, I signed the papers for the loan— but the money wouldn't last long.

Meanwhile, I had been winning national awards and had established name recognition in the entrepreneurial world. I had supporters in very high places, and this had opened doors for me, including access to capital. When this came to Preston's attention, he got greedy and set about to build his own empire based on my relationships and connections.

Before I knew it he had built a large business without my knowledge. He coerced me into personally guaranteeing a $750,000 bank note for expansion. The loan was based on my business reputation and personal credit scores. I didn't want to be saddled with debt. I had been taught to operate in the "what if"—what if he couldn't pay it back? At closing I told him that I wanted to reconsider, that this was too much for me to wrap my mind around. He hissed into my ear that I should have said something sooner. "Just sign the damn papers," he muttered as his face grew red.

Reluctantly, I signed the loan and hoped for the best. I hated myself for being so spineless. I had every right to say no: I was more than 50 percent of the equation because it was my credit rating, relationships, and reputation that had qualified us for the loan. I dug my own grave the day I agreed to sign a personal guarantee.

Almost as soon as the money hit my company's bank account, he started redirecting the funds into his anemic corporate account. While my company started to flounder from lack of operating capital, his started to soar. I walked around holding my breath, praying he would honor his debt to the bank. To the contrary, he started living large—picking up tabs at the country club and passing out undeserved bonuses like food stamps. When I asked questions, he would become enraged, knowing I would back down. I was too petrified to fully acknowledge the gravity of my financial and emotional abuse. Instead, I made an art of convincing myself to trust him.

I did not keep my eye on the status of the loan repayment as I should have because I couldn't bear to embrace the "what if" that was becoming reality. It wasn't long before the line of credit was used up, and he was defaulting on repayment. That's when my husband fled the scene and left me to figure out how to make good on his loan default.

The bank that had given us the $750,000 loan had made it clear that if they could not get repayment from him, they would get it out of me, one way or another. By then, the penalties and interest had escalated into a note in excess of $1 million. I retained legal counsel to help me navigate through this ambush. Above all, I wanted to make sure that I did everything I could to avoid the unthinkable: bankruptcy.

When the loan accelerated, the bank didn't care that I was a struggling single parent. The bank didn't care that I was physically and mentally exhausted, or that I had an honest heart and good intentions when I stood by my man thinking I could help him make his dreams come true. The bank didn't care about me as a person. They wanted their money and I was the low-hanging fruit.

I finally decided that since neither the bank nor my ex-husband cared about what happened to me and my children, it was time to slay my own dragons. I had hit the proverbial brick wall, and it put my fear in perspective. I picked up the phone, called my attorney and told him to file for bankruptcy.

The next morning, I showed up at my attorney's office to sign my financial death certificate. There was no turning back. I wandered mindlessly across the parking lot and walked into a Denny's to eat breakfast. All of a sudden, I was famished.

I ordered the Grand Slam. It was the most food I could get for the five dollars I had in the back pocket of my black jeans. My calm vanished as I thought about my ex's "grand slam" lifestyle that had caused my financial ruin. All my life, I had worked to pay my bills, and there I sat at Denny's while he was probably at a Ritz-Carlton somewhere basking in the sun with a woman young enough to be his daughter. I laid the money on the table and walked out. I had lost my appetite.

At the public hearing for my bankruptcy case, the trustee read my case to an audience of strangers. She wanted to know why I thought I should be allowed to remain in a 6,000 square foot house and drive a luxury car. She waged a campaign to make me look as bad as my ex-husband. But I had already lost my dignity, my business credibility, and my credit score; nothing was going to rock me anymore. Throughout the hearing, I thought, *Bring it on. I did nothing wrong but love the wrong man.*

Current Snapshot

The threats that the bankruptcy trustee made to destroy me never materialized. My bankruptcy was granted in record time, there were no additional investigations, and the bank stopped calling. The actual recovery from bankruptcy was not pretty. When I needed to purchase a car, the best interest rate I could negotiate was 14.5 percent for a car I didn't even like. The mortgage company would not accept my personal checks for six months, even though I had never missed a payment. All the while, I had to keep telling myself, *This too shall pass.*

It has been six years now. I recently pulled up my credit score and found that it was much better than I feared. My ex-husband continues to live in complete denial of the havoc he wreaked on me. To clear his conscience, however, over the past few years he started throwing our kids bones—a car here, a shopping spree there—all the things I can't afford to do for them. I don't even try to compete with his checkbook. Dirty money never washes clean. In the meantime, I am making daily deposits into my spiritual, health, and love account, making sure that no one can ever bankrupt the bank of me again.

Pearls of Wisdom.....

From "The Grand Slam"

- Do not sign a personal guarantee unless it is fueling your dreams and you are completely willing to lose all your assets if things don't go as expected.
- If your spouse tries to bully you into signing or cosigning on a loan that you are not comfortable with, and it is obvious he does not have your best interest at heart, call an attorney and seek protection.
- Keep an eye on your finances at all times. Do not naïvely entrust them to anyone, not even your husband. You have a responsibility to yourself and to any minor dependents to understand anything and everything financial that could affect you.
- If declaring bankruptcy becomes inevitable, do it sooner rather than later, so you can start to rebuild your financial life as quickly as possible. If you are forced to file for

bankruptcy, align yourself with a financial advisor or credit expert who can help you rebuild your credit as quickly as possible.

CORONER'S REPORT ON FINANCIAL ABUSE

RICK LINDSEY, **Managing Partner of Covenant Wealth Management, LLC**

The stories of financial abuse portrayed in this section all have a familiar ring to them. The most common theme that resonates among spouses experiencing financial abuse is intimidation and deception. In "On a Moment's Notice," Darla experienced this in a monumental way. I wonder what would have happened if she had refused to go to the bank to sign for the loan. Her husband probably would have backed down, which would have forced open the line of communication. If her husband continued to pressure her, she might have seen the writing on the wall and cut her losses sooner, seeking the protection of the courts. No one has the right to back you against a wall, not even a spouse. That is blackmail, and most assuredly a form of emotional and financial abuse.

I can't tell you how many times I've spoken with women who say that they have no idea where the money goes every month. I cannot stress enough how important it is for both spouses to be fully engaged in all of the financial aspects of their marriage.

I've met more than one husband who likes to boast that he is the "man of the house" and doesn't feel he has to discuss every decision he makes with his wife. My response is, "As the man of the house, you should want your wife to be aware of everything about the household finances. If something unexpected happens to you, how well will she be able to make decisions going forward if she has limited knowledge of what you've been doing for the past several months or years?"

Most of the time, that statement drives the point home, and the "man of the house" softens his stance and agrees that he needs to do a better job of educating his wife about the finances of their household. However, on those occasions when the husband still refuses to change his attitude about including his wife in the financial decisions, I know right then that they are headed for trouble and/or divorce.

A very common red flag that signals financial abuse to me is when the wife is afraid to speak up and voice her opinion. She defers every question to her husband for fear of saying something that he will not like. This is a very obvious indicator of intimidation. Whether intentional or unintentional, this kind of behavior is the fallout from a combination of emotional and financial abuse.

In "Beating the Odds," Pam struggled to protect the financial assets of her elderly family members while trying to hold on to her frayed marriage. No well-meaning spouse should have backed her into a corner like this. It is usually the woman who has the desire to avoid conflict, even if it means subduing her natural instincts about right and wrong. Men will often take full advantage of this fact. I tell my clients that if it doesn't feel like the right move for both of you, then the answer is to stand still. No one should have to live in a world of ethical conflict and financial strife, especially not when they have been brought about by a spouse.

Beauty and the Creep

Emotional Abuse

As a child I used to chant "Sticks and stones may break my bones but words can never hurt me." As an adult I have learned that nothing could be further from the truth.

"What are you, an idiot?"

"I must have been crazy when I decided to marry you."

"You are so damn cheap you can't even buy the right trash bags. Can't you do anything right?"

"You call yourself an MBA? My secretary has more intelligence than you!"

"I don't know why I wasted my money to give you a birthday party; you are worthless."

Having been on the receiving end of strong words both positive and negative, I can personally attest that the tongue can reinforce and it can also be lethal. Inside my childhood home I was blessed to receive words of affirmation, love, and support. When my husband verbally attacked me after we were married, I was caught off guard. I was not trained in verbal combat, so I retreated and began to berate myself as well. I did not defend myself against this rhetorical bully. Instead, criticizing my subordinates became my weapon of choice, my way of swinging back at my husband. I also became obsessed with gaining his approval. I wore myself out trying to figure out ways to please him so that I would feel affirmed.

One of the reasons my former husband and I get along so well now is that I don't care what he thinks about me. I have given myself permission to be just who I am. Besides, if he even starts to raise his voice, or hints that he is going to make an insulting comment, I shut him down. I remind him that he can't talk to me in a condescending manner, suggest that we pick up the conversation when he is calm, and—if all else fails and the conversation is over the phone—I hang up on him. I have learned to set boundaries and I do not allow him to get remotely close to crossing the line. I have vowed never to let anyone disrespect me or control me with their mouth or actions again.

Eleanor Roosevelt was right on point when she said, "No one has the power to make you feel inferior without your consent." This has become the mantra by which I live. Striving to develop an attitude of humility like the biblical Jabez in 1 Chronicles 4:9-10, I pray daily that I will not inflict pain on anyone. Every time I open my mouth I try to do a sound check, asking myself, "Will the words that I am about to speak uplift or tear down? Destroy or build up? Teach or distract?"

Emotional abuse and verbal abuse are Siamese twins, conjoined in a spirit of destruction. It is difficult for one to move without the other. The verbal put-downs and threats pull triggers that negatively affect the psyche of their target.

They evoke fear and self-doubt. They could be considered the most insidious forms of abuse because, just like carbon monoxide, you can't see them, but before you know it, they can kill you.

Verbal abuse is almost always the precursor to other types of abuse, including physical, sexual, and financial. Verbal abusers are the worst kind of cowards because they hide their crime so well. Unlike physical, sexual, or financial abuse, unless someone else is in earshot, verbal abuse leaves no evidence of affliction except for what lingers in the minds of its victims, sometimes for years. In this next chapter you will witness how verbal and emotional abuse can catch even the most accomplished woman off guard and cause her to temporarily second-guess her worth.

Death and life are in the power of the tongue.
—Proverbs 18:21

Birthday Blues: Joyce
Cause of Death: Infidelity and Emotional Abandonment

Sex is a privilege of marriage. It is God's creation and intended as a gift to the couple. Mark and I spent a lot of time enjoying that gift in our marriage. Yet even though we set off sparks in the bedroom, our relationship was void of intimacy. Sex was essentially a release of tension for us, not the basis for a strong and caring connection.

Over time, we talked less and less, and Mark slowly shut me out of every aspect of his world. He came to regard his employees as his family—not the children and me. I despised him for not loving us the way he should and despised his employees for getting the loyalty and attention I craved. It was hard to ignore the long hours he spent at the office, the spontaneous business trips with his assistant, the receipts for clothes and jewelry that

I never received, and, most telling of all, his waning desire to have sex with me. I knew we were in trouble.

The more he withdrew from me, the more I tried to rekindle the romance in our marriage. I obsessed over keeping my body in shape, my hair fashionably styled, the house in order, and the children well scrubbed and behaved. Still, his time away from home stretched out more and more. When he came home at night, he read his paper, watched television, and escaped into his own little world in his study, leaving us in an empty space void of a husband or father. Typically, while he was winding down around 9:00 p.m., I would just be gearing up for an evening of checking homework, giving baths, clearing the kitchen table, and attending to everyone's needs but my own. On the weekends, he was often away playing golf or attending to "business matters."

When my birthday came one particular year, I decided he had ignored me one time too many. I asked what we were doing to celebrate, and he responded he planned to go boating with the gang (his employees) and had not planned anything special for me.

I felt ignored, uncelebrated, and unloved.

I was desperate to feel appreciated, and it just so happened that my ex-fiancé, Westin, was in town on business. I returned his phone call and made my own secret plans. I arranged for the children to go to a friend's house while I visited my friend at his five-star hotel.

In the privacy of his suite, we embraced warmly and caught each other up on our equally miserable marriages. We had both been pushed away by selfish spouses who barely acknowledged our existence. We escaped into each other's arms, but we did not have intercourse; luckily, my menstrual cycle saved us from doing what was in both of our minds. Instead we kissed and held onto each other as if our lives depended on it. We snuggled in bed, watched TV, and ordered room service. Westin said he felt like our souls were married that night, but I knew that was not the truth in God's eyes. Late that evening I left reluctantly, feeling loved but very guilty. We had journeyed to a very dangerous place.

After that, I became preoccupied with thoughts of Westin. I fantasized about him making love to me the way we had before we married other people. Before we knew it, we had rekindled a full-blown love affair. It was more passionate than ever before. We became each other's lifeline. We would talk often, sometimes ten times a day, the way teenagers do. We rationalized our adulterous behavior by exercising our sense of entitlement, telling ourselves that our respective spouses did not love us the way we deserved.

Once the passion overtook us, we started doing irrational and reckless things. We took turns catching a flight in the middle of the workday to meet at a hotel to have sex. We would shower, dress, and travel back to our horrible lives to be home in time for dinner or other family obligations. I began to hate myself for living a dual life.

Westin's wife was bipolar and mean-spirited. He didn't want to leave the marriage because they had a very young son, and he wanted to be part of his son's daily life. Being intimate with Westin was a double-edged sword, my greatest source of joy but also my greatest source of pain. Guilt overshadowed my loneliness, and I began to feel empty again. Miserable in both situations, I decided to abruptly end both the affair and my marriage.

Current Snapshot

Even though my husband had been cheating on me throughout our marriage, and even though our marriage was beyond repair when my affair first began with Westin, I still had no right to engage in an adulterous affair. It may sound cliché, but two wrongs will never make a right. I asked God for forgiveness for my affair and have moved on with my life.

Westin remains the kindest, dearest man I've ever known. In my mind, he will always be my soul mate. I keep my distance from him now because I don't want to interfere in his marriage any more than I already have. I made the wrong decision when I chose not to marry him, and know that now he will never be mine. I am in love with another wonderful man now and hope to remarry soon.

Pearls of Wisdom......

From "Birthday Blues"

- No one wins in adultery, and someone will always get hurt.
- Adultery is always a temporary solution to a long-term problem, and it is always wrong.
- Your husband's bad behavior does not give you a green light to take up the same adulterous actions.
- The inevitable breakup that stems from an adulterous relationship can make you feel much worse than you did before it began.
- Ultimately, no other person can fill the emptiness in your heart. Contentment must first come from within.

HER OWN WORST ENEMY: TAILOR
Cause of Death: Drug Addiction, Financial and Emotional Abuse

Some time after my first marriage failed, a mutual friend introduced me to Brad. He seemed to have the whole package; he was handsome, successful, easy to talk to, supportive of my career, and, most importantly, appeared interested in the well-being of my young daughter, Chelsea. We had a relatively brief courtship. He and his young daughter had been deserted by his ex-wife. The two girls got along well, and in no time we had married and blended our families with ease.

Even though we both had homes already, we decided that we wanted to build a new house to accommodate our expanded family. He insisted that I sell my house and put the proceeds into a joint account. It was not until much later that I found out the equity from the sale of his house had been tucked away into his private portfolio.

Things started to spiral downward quickly. My husband was not the great guy that I thought I had married.

He was moody and selfish—and a controlling bully toward me. He bought himself toys whenever he wanted them, such as a boat, motorcycle, and truck. According to him, his money was his to spend. His focus was on his own pleasure—always. I was left to worry about the well-being of both our daughters on my own.

Both of the girls had big holes in their hearts after being abandoned by one of their parents. I wanted to make sure that Brad and I made them feel happy, whole, and secure. From the beginning, I treated Brad's daughter, Samantha, as if she were my own. I made a point to attend all her school and extracurricular activities. I wanted to be sure I never let Samantha down. I was trying to compensate for the damage her mother had caused.

Brad did not reciprocate with Chelsea. In the ten years of our marriage, he attended maybe two of her activities. This crushed her. She was needy for a father figure, and continued to worship him. When he came home in the evenings, she would run to the door to greet him, but he seemed to look right through her. I would try to compensate for his coldness by telling her that he was just tired. The profound sadness in her eyes told me that she knew otherwise.

Then Brad's mother entered our world like a pit bull. Before I knew it, she was living with us. I was not consulted about this decision, not even informed until the day she moved in. She always had plenty of unsolicited advice for me, and seemed to find fault in the way that I did practically everything.

Brad took to calling me names and insulting me right in front of her. No matter how bad his behavior was, she did not flinch. He let her know that he had no respect for me, which gave her the green light to verbally abuse me as well. On the flip side, he always told me to keep my "nosy" parents out of "his" house. According to him, all they did was meddle. My parents, understanding the pressure I was under, did not interfere even though they had been all but shut out of my life. They tried to help me any way they could—from a distance—and kept their comments to themselves.

By day, I ran a staff of over forty architects. By night, I was a frightened slave to my husband's whims, and served as his maid, cook, and concubine. I often found myself on my hands and knees scrubbing floors and toilets after a twelve-hour workday. Brad hated a dirty house. Although his mother lived with us, she never picked up a broom or bucket. She would cook on occasion, but only for herself. Family meals were my responsibility. She did not even help with her own grandchild.

Brad never hit me, but his words slapped me over and over again. He called me everything under the sun, from an ignorant ingrate to a cheating slut. I didn't know when he thought I had the time to conduct an affair. I was too busy taking care of everybody but myself.

He was always on edge, so I was always on edge. I was constantly afraid to set off a trigger in him. About a year into the marriage, I made the mistake of sharing with his mother that I suspected he might be on drugs. He had lost a significant amount of weight, which was coupled with increased mood swings and a very volatile temper. He would sometimes come home from "business" trips with glassy eyes, and frequently acted paranoid.

Brad's mother told me rather nonchalantly "He's been fighting an addiction problem for years. I thought that when he married you, his life would turn around. Apparently, that isn't working out." She then asked me to make a pact with her: the first time that I suspected he was using again, I was supposed to hide the car keys from him and call her. She said we would "work this out together." I should have known better.

Not long after our heart to heart, I called her and said I was sure Brad was high. She cursed me and told me I was ruining her life by telling her this. She said it was inconsiderate of me to share my speculations and lay this burden on her.

It was very clear to me then that he had inherited his craziness from her. There I was, married to a drug addict and saddled with a resentful, manipulative mother-in-law. The worst thing about the situation was that I had dragged my innocent daughter into this dangerous environment.

The only thing I knew to do at that point was to go into overdrive hoping to make things work. I thought that if I worked harder, smiled more, cleaned the house until it was spotless, and gave him all the sex he demanded, then his demons would go away and our lives would resemble normalcy.

One night I came home exceptionally exhausted. Brad was in a rare form. He was in a good mood and commented that he was happy to have an "empty nest" since his daughter had recently gone off to college. My daughter, however, was only eleven. I couldn't believe that he thought he could behave as if she didn't exist. I had supported his daughter through her formative years—now what about mine? That night I found myself on the bathroom floor crying uncontrollably. I had finally hit rock bottom.

The next day, I casually asked Chelsea how she would feel if we did not live with Brad anymore. She told me that she wouldn't miss him because she had never had a father in her life. While this pained me, her statement also gave me the courage to do what I should have done a long time ago. Within the week, I left Brad, taking only my most prized treasure, Chelsea, with me. We moved to a modest apartment. The sudden upheaval of my life initially forced us to live from paycheck to paycheck. However, I do not regret my decision, and would do it all over again if I had to.

Current Snapshot

Chelsea is now in college and is an excellent student. She is destined for great things because she believes in herself and will never allow a man to jeopardize her self-love. We both learned that lesson from Brad. I feel very blessed that she has turned out so well, considering the struggles of her childhood.

Brad has since been on a campaign to win me back. At times, I feel lonely and vulnerable, and almost wish I could believe that he has changed, but I love myself too much to take that chance.

Pearls of Wisdom.....

From "Her Own Worst Enemy"

- No price is too high to pay for happiness and sanity.
- Your spouse does not have a right to spend your money unilaterally without your consent, and you need to revoke your consent if you suspect he may be using your paycheck to fund his drug addiction.
- Stay true to your deepest values. Money and comfort are not as important as your safety and sense of self-worth.

DOCTOR TRIPOLAR: EILEEN
Cause of Death: Verbal and Physical Abuse

Jared and I met when I was a medical student in North Carolina and he was an intern at the affiliated medical school hospital. However, it was not a student-mentor association that brought us together, but a doctor-patient relationship that began when I was hospitalized for pneumonia. Our paths had previously never crossed, but while he was managing my health we found we had a mutual group of friends. I was charmed by his work ethic, intelligence, and humility, and impressed that he had risen from extremely humble beginnings and worked very hard to arrive at this professional apex.

After my second year of medical school, it became apparent that my heart was not in my studies. I struggled with my third year, and finally made the decision to take a break from school. As I was preparing to pack up my apartment and head back to California, Jared proposed in typical Jared fashion: Over the phone, he said, "Hey, you wanna get married?" We were married two days later in a small, semiformal ceremony and purchased a house two weeks after that. I was pregnant with our first child by our first wedding anniversary.

By that time, Jared was finishing his second year in a private practice position he had accepted in a very rural town about an hour away. He received a lot of criticism for going to such a small, unincorporated town, but the practice turned out to be a gold mine. His patients adored him, and all the naysayers had to eat their words.

While Jared was not arrogant, he was definitely a moody person. The cloud of being in love had helped me overlook this while we were dating, but he could literally walk out of one room and into another, emerging with a sudden attitude of anger and spewing expletives. I never knew which Jared was going to show his face. He was both brilliant and roguish, funny and mean, charming and hurtful. His mood swings were worse than bipolar, and in my head I started to refer to him as "tripolar."

I tried very hard to embrace all of Jared's personalities. He would start arguments, and many times the subject matter didn't even make sense to me. When his anger rose to the pinnacle of rage, I was often crying. He would usually end up apologizing, but the damage had been done. I was never one to back down or be submissive, but I learned quickly to pick my arguments and let some things go.

Over time, if he did not get a reaction from me (in the form of argument, crying, or hurt feelings), he upped the anger and rage. His words and actions drove a wedge between us that cooled down things in the bedroom. The majority of his anger then came from my reluctance to have sex with him. For me, however, it was difficult to be intimate with someone who brutalized your soul.

We went for counseling, and the therapist was amazed at how long I had stayed in such a malignant relationship.

He suspected that Jared was bipolar, but when he suggested further treatment, Jared rose from his seat, insulted the therapist, and walked out. Eventually it became clear to me, however, that multiple personalities resided in Jared. On a rare day he was supportive; on a normal day, he made it a sport to tear down my world.

Over four years of marriage, we had three daughters. I was the typical soccer mom—huge van, PTA meetings, and all. Jared, however, had no father figure to emulate since he was raised by a single mother. Often I had to set the stage for father/daughter events, but he would usually rise to the occasion. He loved his girls—that much I knew for certain.

Jared's practice quickly flew off the charts in terms of patient volume and income generation. I provided the business understanding I had picked up watching my own mother manage my father's private practice, and Jared provided the medical care. Before he was thirty, he and I had worked together to establish a million-dollar practice in a remote town outside of Raleigh. The locals in the town where he practiced loved him. When he gained attention from Time magazine and other national media for being the heroic country doctor, his humility and civility flew the coop.

I didn't know from one moment to the next what kind of mood he would be in. Given his impressive collection of hunting rifles, I didn't want to do anything to provoke him, even though it seemed at times that everything I did or said was an irritant to him. He knew that I was committed to the marriage and had my hands full with all the children's activities, running the office, and entertaining his colleagues, but he would routinely threaten to file for divorce. He knew this terrified me, which was entertaining to him.

The emotional abuse soon escalated to physical abuse, but for years I continued to tolerate it, until one day my oldest daughter actually witnessed her father pulling me onto the floor by my hair. A few weeks later, she woke up to find that her father had kicked in the bathroom door when I had locked it behind me in an attempt to escape more physical abuse. This kind of abuse was sporadic compared to the emotional abuse, but I was concerned about protecting my daughters from witnessing any more of the violence.

To escape the craziness I began to routinely visit my mother in California for the summer with the girls. It was an opportunity for me to take a vacation from fear. At times I would hyperventilate prior to boarding the plane to return back to the war zone. Despite the abuse, my mother, out of her old-school mentality, continued to encourage me to stay with my husband—for better or for worse. The final straw didn't come until he called me in California one day and blurted out the question that was not rare for him to pose: "What are we going to do about our messed-up marriage?"

This time, rather than getting upset and crying as I usually did, I confidently told him to think of three ways to improve our marriage. I said I would do the same, and we would talk again in two days. I called him back in twenty-four hours, which shocked him, and told him I could only think of one way to improve, which shocked him even more: we needed to get a divorce.

There had been plenty of times he had threatened me with divorce, but this was the first time I had ever mentioned my own desire for such a separation. This time, I knew it was my decision, not something he could force upon me. I was prepared. I sat the girls down, gently explained what was going to happen, and reassured them that we were going to be just fine.

When I finally filed for divorce, Jared went berserk, but by then I didn't care because I could see the light on the horizon. When he left, I decided to get ahead of the gossip curve, knowing all too well how much words could hurt. I strategically began telling people that we were getting a divorce. Each time there was more confidence in my voice. People were going to find out anyway, and I wanted them to hear it from me. One of my dear friends teasingly said to me, "Your divorce is not even fun to gossip about, because you are telling everyone everything, so there are no whispers!" We both laughed; she was right.

Current Snapshot

My daughters adjusted well to our new lifestyle. While they were still in high school, I went back to school myself and earned two master's degrees. I am now gainfully employed by a large health care company in California. I have moved up the corporate ladder quickly and am about where I would be financially if I had worked during what I now refer to as "my other life."

Thanks to a school-related website, an old friend of mine from junior high school found me. We dated for two years and have now been married for three. We have six daughters between the two of us and a comfortable home in Los Angeles almost walking distance from all of our parents. My new husband is a manager with another large company in the area that he has been with for over twenty-six years. I love the stability and have finally found peace of mind.

Pearls of Wisdom.....

From "Doctor Tripolar"

- Verbal abuse is just as detrimental as physical abuse. Neither should be tolerated.
- A person's family background says a lot about the dynamics they can be expected to establish in their own family. When you are about to commit to someone for the rest of your life, you need to do what it takes to make sure you know if they are emotionally stable and have a healthy idea of what family should look like.
- When a spouse shows clear evidence of multiple personalities, professional medical attention is imperative.
- Intelligence and a strong work ethic are not synonymous with kindness and emotional stability.

CORONER'S REPORT ON EMOTIONAL ABUSE

Dr. Yolanda Bruce Brooks, Clinical Psychologist

"Mike, I really want to try and work this out. What can we do?" Sheila asked.

Her husband laughed and turned his back on her in bed, replying in disgust, "You can start by losing fifty pounds."

What is emotional abuse?

The dialogue above from Tyler Perry's popular movie *Why Did I Get Married?* would qualify as emotional abuse. Mike's words tore Sheila apart when she was most vulnerable and desperate, wanting to fix her marriage more than anything else. When a person is verbally attacked on an issue that she values, such as her looks, weight, parenting skills, professional pursuits, and ambitions, this is emotional abuse. How many women in real life have been scarred by such remarks as, "You're too fat"?

Emotional abuse cuts to the core and causes insecurity, despair, and eventually self-hatred. Just as an aggressor uses a weapon to stun or wound, a victimizer may use emotional abuse to gain power, break a person's spirit, or alter their behavior. It frequently begins with a raised voice and escalates to verbal attacks. In other instances, silence or a look of disgust can be just as powerful a tool as a sharp tongue.

Emotional abuse is one of the most treacherous forms of abuse. Some say it is worse than physical because of the lingering impact on the victim's psyche and confidence. Words not only hurt, they kill one's spirit, confidence, and dreams.

You have to be strong to survive verbal attacks. Emotional and financial abuse may not have outward signs, but they can often be far more devastating and much slower to heal than the scars from physical abuse. Its victims are too embarrassed to admit that they could have been so vulnerable, or that they didn't recognize the signs.

To make sure that you know what emotional abuse looks like, here's a checklist.

Signs of Emotional Abuse

- Verbal insult/assault
- Emotional intimidation
- Overt criticism
- Private or public humiliation
- Name-calling
- Chronic raised voice (screaming or yelling)
- Mind games
- Demands to be waited on
- Intimidation (through harsh tone of voice)
- Angry looks or stares
- Criticism of parenting skills

- Refusal to contribute to housework or childcare
- Requiring that partner ask permission to use personal property
- Accusations that partner pays too much attention to someone or something else
- Demands that partner beg for forgiveness
- Ignoring partner
- Pressuring partner to change physical appearance
- Telling partner no one else would want her
- Threatening to take children away
- Driving recklessly to scare partner

Never Never Land

Secrets, Lies, and Addictions

We all have secrets that will go to the grave with us. For some a lifelong secret manifests itself as a love child who shows up at a funeral to cash in on the life insurance policy. For another it might be a gambling habit. As hurtful and shocking as these secrets might be, the offenses are not life-threatening. Most people have some bad habit that could escalate into an addiction if they are not careful, whether it's eating, shopping, gossiping, or smoking. However, drug and alcohol abuse are not secrets that we can ever afford to bury.

Now that I am old enough to connect the dots, I fully understand the correlation between substance abuse and physical abuse. I grew up thinking that my extended family portrait was picture-perfect. What I didn't know as a child was that my cousin and aunt were victimized by the violence of a raging alcoholic. Later in life, I would come to learn that my "favorite uncle" had even threatened to kill my mother with a gun because—you guessed it—he was drunk. I am grateful that my childhood was not tainted by learning about these family secrets during my youthful innocence.

Lies, bad habits, and addictions—everything that happens in the dark will eventually come to light. When a spouse is wed to a bottle, needle, pipe, or pill, they have wandered off into a very dangerous and private world that will eventually undermine the marriage covenant.

In my opinion, drug and alcohol addiction is the worst kind of mistress there is and horrifies me the most, especially after I learned of my own mother's close call. You need only turn on the news or open up a newspaper and you will learn of sports figures and mechanics, politicians and bus drivers who indulge a dangerous habit that wreaks havoc and tears families apart.

Once the unpredictable poison is in their systems, addicts are guaranteed to become irresponsible and irrational. They also have a tendency to demonstrate aggressive behavior that can become very violent. Should you suspect or can validate that your spouse is addicted to drugs or alcohol, it is time to take action and seek help.

Few women want to admit that they married a man who has alcohol or drug addictions. Their first instinct is to go into denial mode, pretending that the disease does not exist. Don't play coy in order to avoid an argument. I once ran across a woman well into her sixties who had been married to an addict for over forty years. I cannot begin to imagine how emotionally exhausting it must have been to be bound to him and all of his lies for as long as she was. No wonder she was working as hard as she was; retirement was not even a remote option in light of his spending habits. I also met a flight attendant whose husband, left to watch their small children, was arrested at their home for drug possession and dealing while she was in midair. Had it not been for a quick-thinking neighbor, Child Protective Services would have taken custody of their children. Shortly you will learn how even a health care professional can overlook the mood swings and aggressive behavior of her highly successful but addicted husband.

The addict's entire life revolves around getting his next drink or fix, and he will do whatever it takes to get it—even if it means pawning your wedding ring or spending the monthly mortgage payment or your children's college fund. Your family's financial livelihood will always be in jeopardy when addictive behavior is part of the equation.

When your spouse keeps secrets that can challenge your livelihood and the safety of your family, he has left you alone to navigate the relationship through a fog of deceit and unforeseen negative consequences. You may not be able to prevent the emotional suicide that arises from your spouse's path of destruction, but you can prevent a murder/suicide. Get the spiritual guidance and professional help you need for your spouse and yourself, or before you know it, you will be a codependent struggling to hang on to an imitation of life.

CUT YOUR LOSSES: JUSTINE
Cause of Death: Concealed Paternity,

Emotional Abandonment

I always knew that I wanted to get married someday, but marriage was not high on my to-do list. After I graduated from college, I went on to law school. During my twenties, I focused on building my career as a criminal prosecutor. I was fortunate enough to be made a criminal court judge when I was barely thirty years old. At this point, I felt my career was fairly well established, and I decided to start entertaining the notion of marriage.

I first met Brian on a blind date. He was so funny and charming, and I loved that he made me laugh. I found his humor to be a pleasant and much-appreciated departure from my routine days of hearing about violence, assault, and murder while sitting on the bench.

We were both in criminal justice jobs. He was a probation officer and had a good understanding of the dynamics and pressures of my profession. My much higher status as a judge did not seem to bother him in the least. He always told me how proud he was of me, and seemed to enjoy the privileges my title often afforded us. We attended galas, were regulars on VIP lists, and never waited in lines at restaurants. He blended easily into my social circle. When we became engaged, no one except my dad seemed surprised. When Brian asked my father for my hand in marriage, he told Brian that the marriage would never work.

"I know the way I have raised her," my father said. "She is very ambitious, and I just can't see that you are right for her."

I was hurt by my father's lack of confidence in the man I had chosen to marry, but I continued to plan my wedding. The night before our wedding, however, I received a phone call at my home from a strange woman. She told me that I should think twice about my impending wedding, and asked if I knew that my soon-to-be husband had fathered her baby. I was stunned by her words and didn't know what to think. When I confronted him later that night, Brian denied the accusation. Apart from the strange phone call, I had no reason to think that Brian had ever deceived me. The wedding proceeded as planned.

It wasn't until a year after the wedding that the mysterious woman's accusations came back to haunt me. An attorney friend of mine called asking me to remind Brian that his paternity hearing was at ten the next morning and that it was important for him to be on time. My friend apparently had assumed that I was in the loop on the issue. The timing of this revelation could not have been worse; I was up for reelection as a judge, and I did not need any negative publicity. Because he had not been helping with the baby, the baby's mother had decided to make noise when she learned that Brian was marrying a prominent judge. The paternity test proved positive, and the judge ordered him to pay child support. After this, my trust level for Brian dissipated. Not only had he kept a love child hidden from me, his lack of interest in her was an undeniable character flaw that could not be ignored.

We had two beautiful daughters together, and my work continued to go well, but Brian was apparently incapable of growing up. He was self-absorbed and obsessed with his hobbies. He would spend his last dollar on his race car and neglect household expenses. I kept the household running using my own money, and whenever he attempted to pay me back, his checks bounced.

The morning of our four-year-old's birthday party, he went off to work on his race car instead of helping with preparations. He promised to be back for the party, which turned out to be another lie. Brian came home at ten o'clock that night, long after the candles had been blown out, the presents unwrapped, and the guests had left. He expected me to understand and smooth the matter over with our daughter, but I couldn't get over the hurt look that appeared on my daughter's face when she realized that her father was not coming to her party.

I finally understood at that moment that I needed to cut my losses. Brian, of course, didn't want to get a divorce. Few would want to give up the lifestyle I had provided for him. But I no longer cared what he wanted.

Once we divorced, Brian barely managed to pay the same amount of child support for our two daughters that the other woman would receive for one child. Luckily I was making enough money on my own, so our lifestyle never suffered. What I could not buy was a responsible father for my girls. They rarely saw Brian. The hardest thing for them to deal with was his perpetually broken promises. He would call them and get them all excited about going somewhere with him. They would pack their bags and wait by the door, but he would never show up. His lies broke their hearts time and time again. I never felt the need to badmouth Brian to the girls. They were more than capable of drawing their own conclusions about their father.

When our youngest graduated from high school, Brian finally hammered the nail into his own coffin. He took the two girls to lunch and handed them both a slip of paper. He said that he had opened savings accounts for each of them with a starting balance of $1,000. They came home excited and told me all about it. I hoped for their sakes that he had changed and was telling them the truth.

A few weeks later, my oldest daughter suggested that she and her sister go to the bank to check on their accounts before they left for college. A banking officer confirmed that their father had set up accounts for them, and informed them that they each had a balance of ten dollars. The two extra zeros were nothing more than another of their father's lies.

Current Snapshot

I have never remarried, but I am happier today than I was being married to Brian. I remain open to remarriage if the right person ever comes along. I've accepted that sometimes you have to kiss a lot of frogs before you find the prince.

My daughters are doing extremely well. They are both pursuing graduate degrees and are beautiful inside and out. The three of us are very close, and I am grateful that they have never given me a day of trouble. We have been fortunate in that several of my friends' husbands are very supportive of us. They have served as male role models for the girls over the years.

Pearls of Wisdom......

From "Cut Your Losses"

- The truth will always come out. When it does, you must be prepared to take action.
- Do not badmouth your ex. The children will find out just what they need to know in their own time, and will draw their own conclusions. Do what you can to protect them, but don't succumb to petty blame games.
- A man who does not accept the responsibility of any child he fathered is bad news.
- If your child's father is missing in action, try to find other male role models to fill that void.

I Love You to Death: Susan
Cause of Death: Drug Abuse, Aggressive Stalking,

My first husband and I divorced when my son, Ryan, was twelve years old. Even though Ryan's father paid child support, he was an absentee father. At that point in my life, I made a conscious decision to focus on raising Ryan. I told myself I would not consider a serious relationship until he was in college.

Seemingly right on schedule, I met my future husband, Larry, only months after Ryan left for college. Mutual friends of ours thought that we would be a good match. We dated for three months and then married. I was not looking for a father for my son. I had already raised him by myself. I felt it was time to focus on me.

Larry was charming, handsome, and smart. As a bonus, he was a highly-sought-after architect who earned over half a million dollars a year. I did not marry him for his money, but it was nice to have a financial reprieve after years of struggling to provide for Ryan on my own. Larry even wanted me to stop working, but I kept my job as a nurse. I felt more comfortable maintaining my own income—just in case.

It wasn't long before I began to suspect that Larry was being unfaithful. Sometimes when I answered the phone at the house, the person on the other end would hang up as soon as they heard my voice. If I walked in the room while he was on the phone, his conversations would suddenly become hushed and stilted. When my female friends came over to the house, he exuded an aura that made me feel awkward. I discussed these things with my closest friends, but they encouraged me to hang in there.

"The man is basically a millionaire," they reasoned, as if that made up for any other potential flaws. But I was content with our comfortable life, and besides, like my friends said, "All men cheat, anyway. Don't they?" Deep inside, however, I knew that I was staying in the marriage for the wrong reasons. I was compromising my core values and for something as potentially fleeting as companionship and financial security.

I ignored my need for emotional stability and physical safety as his behavior became volatile. He had told me that he had been raised in a dysfunctional family and that his father had beaten his mother. He said he hated his father for it but equally despised his mother for not fighting back. I rationalized that it wasn't Larry's fault that he was the way he was. He deserved the love of a good woman, I told myself. He confided in me that he prayed that he would never feel compelled to hit me as his father had hit his mother. I told him not to worry, and that, if that happened, I would walk away immediately and permanently remove the temptation.

He started picking verbal fights that sometimes kept me up all night. My job at the hospital was very demanding, and I needed to be well rested to focus and be able to think on my feet. As an emergency room and intensive care nurse, I kept watch over critically ill patients, and their lives were in my hands when I was on duty.

To block out the drama of my home life, I escaped into a world of fantasy through romance novels. One night Larry's rage finally uncorked. He returned home from a business trip and found me reading in bed. He appeared unusually sullen and depressed. He sat down across from our bed and hung his head as tears started rolling down his face. I told him that I didn't know what was bothering him, but that I was sure it would be all right. "It's OK to cry. Just let it out," I said. "Crying is a way for the soul to cleanse itself."

I was sincere, but unknowingly had stoked the fire already raging in him. In a split second, he snapped. He lunged toward me, his eyes wild. In disbelief, I instinctively rolled onto my stomach, face down, and tried to cover my head with pillows. I couldn't believe this was happening to me! I had witnessed the effects of this type of abuse day after day at my job, but had never envisioned myself on the receiving end.

His blows rained down on my body. As I prayed for him to spare my life, I had flashbacks to the numerous faces of women I had helped stitch up over the span of my almost twenty years as a nurse. I had seen victim after victim with their teeth knocked out, jaws and noses broken, faces cut. Many of these women's assailants tried to make their wives or girlfriends undesirable to anyone else by maiming or disfiguring them.

Still under attack, I managed to grab the phone and hit the speed dial for 911. The police arrived shortly. Once an officer had handcuffed Larry, I called my best friend, who also happened to be a no-nonsense lawyer. She rushed right over while the police were still there. Larry was crying, apologizing, and declaring that he would never do such a thing again. All the while, my friend took pictures of my bruised back. Even though the police placed a restraining order on him that night, I was terrified to be in the house alone after that—and for good reason:

After a few weeks, Larry broke in, but, fortunately, I was not home at the time. When I called to confront him, he first denied that he had been in my house, but then shouted that he noticed my tube of diaphragm gel was almost empty. He wanted to know whom I had been sleeping with. I told him that it was not his business, but also that the gel had not been used since he left the house. As soon as I hung up, I reported the trespassing incident to the police.

We divorced not long after, but he continued to stalk me for the next two years. I moved three times within the same metro area, but he found me every time. He camped outside of my house in his car and would sometimes call late at night, often just breathing into the phone. I was a frazzled, paranoid, nervous wreck, always looking over my shoulder. It was impossible for me to live without fear. Finally, the friend who had introduced Larry to me called when he learned that I was being stalked.

"Susan, let me first apologize for not sharing this with you sooner, but I thought you should know, given the way things have turned out: Larry has a very expensive cocaine habit." I was frozen in shock. On one hand, I was relieved to finally be able to rationalize Larry's erratic behavior. On the other hand, I wondered how, as a nurse, I could have overlooked the obvious. I felt stupid, naive, and incompetent. The aggressive behavior, mood swings, depression—the signs were all there, and I had missed it. He'd had a mistress all right.

Current Snapshot

I accepted the reality that our relationship was beyond salvaging the day Larry told me that if he couldn't have me, no one would—that he would kill me first and then kill himself. I believed he could and would do it, and knew I had to do something drastic. I decided to take a former employer and mentor up on an offer he had made almost a year earlier. Dr. Shultz offered me a lifeline by asking me to join his practice in Rhode Island. Finally, my nightmare was over.

About six months after I moved, I picked up the ringing phone and found Larry on the other end. I froze. Somehow, he had found me again and was calling me from a rehab center. As part of his treatment, he needed to apologize to me and admit that he was a drug addict. He said he wanted to reconcile, and claimed he would love me until the day he died. I turned down his offer, thanked him for his honesty, and wished him well. At last, I could bury my horrible life with him and move on.

Once I settled in to my new job, I started visiting friends in Cape Cod on weekends. I rebuilt my financial base, bought a second home on the island, and established a small coffee shop. I am married now for the third time, and, as they say, the third time is the charm. I have retired from nursing, and my husband and I have made our permanent home on the island. I now live a life of peace and joy. What more can I say? It doesn't get any better than this. We will love each other until death parts us.

Pearls of Wisdom......

From "I Love You to Death"

- Love does not work on a timeline. Don't rush to fill an empty nest. True love will wait for you.
- Take all threats—especially death threats—seriously.
- Trust your instincts. Don't allow your desires to overwhelm your perceptions.
- If someone is stalking you, take all the precautions you can. Remove yourself as far from their vicinity as possible.
- Do not let your friends live vicariously through you.

BEWARE SOME DREAMS DO COME TRUE: SPARKLE
Physical Abuse, Emotional Abuse, Infidelity, and Substance Abuse

My ex-husband, Steve, and I both came from impoverished backgrounds. Growing up, I dreamed of escaping to become a superstar like Diana Ross. He wanted to become a famous football player. We met in college, where he was on a athletic scholarship. He was the first person in his family to go to college. I was there because I knew that education was my ticket out of poverty. My mother had been forced to drop out of college because she was pregnant, and I was determined not to do likewise.

When Steve and I started dating, we were lucky if we could scrape up enough money to share a hamburger. Back then, we shared almost everything we had and often laughed at how poor we were. He seemed to be a country boy at heart, and he was always playful and fun to be around.

Before long, Steve made a name for himself among the NFL scouts. In his senior year, his dream came true when he was drafted by the league. Overnight, he became rich, famous, and out of control. He left college as a top draft pick to play with his first professional team.

When he left, our first child was six months old. The baby had not been in our playbook, but I had managed to finish college and Steve promised that he would never leave me. Although he claimed that he would take care of his baby, he didn't want to get married, and I had an uneasy feeling in the pit of my stomach when he left to start training. I was alone, scared, and depressed—just as my mother had been when she first had me. It felt like a generational curse.

After the season started, Steve said that the baby and I could come live with him. When I joined him, I was immediately confronted with a lifestyle I did not want. I found Steve drinking, partying, and surrounded by groupies. Women constantly called the house for him, even though I had moved in. I dealt with it because I loved him and I wanted my baby to know his father.

Then, for the first time in our relationship, he hit me. It took me by surprise, and I hit him back. He told me I should leave and get on with my life, because he neither loved me nor wanted me around. After having been disrespected in every way possible, I decided I deserved better and left.

I was blessed with good looks, so I had confidence that I wouldn't be alone for long, even if I had a young son, and I wasn't. As soon as Steve found out I was dating someone else, he started pursuing me again. He sent me expensive gifts, including a shiny BMW and my own American Express card. My mother cheered him on and encouraged me to turn the other cheek and marry him. The gifts were enticing, and his continued presence in my life reminded me that I did love him. I wanted things to work out with Steve, and I wanted to be married. The absence of a father in my life still haunted me, so I buried the previous mishaps and married Steve at the beginning of his second season in the NFL.

We had all the luxuries that go with football fame: cars, a nanny, a designer wardrobe, and a glamorous social life. We were on TV and in magazines. As part of the athletic elite, we lived a charmed life—or at least it appeared so to the outside world.

Early in our marriage, Steve disappeared for a few days. He didn't call or answer the phone at the apartment where he lived during the season. He seemed to think that the only rules that applied to him were those that counted on the field.

I decided to show up at the apartment unannounced. I let myself in before Steve could disentangle himself from the woman he was holding. I had caught him red-handed. I asked the woman if she knew that Steve was married. She looked at him in shock and nervously rushed to gather up her belongings. I told her to get the hell out before someone got hurt.

Through my tears, I cursed him, throwing things and making threats. Then I made the mistake of staying with him. He told me that I was lucky to be with him. He reminded me that he was rich and famous and that plenty of women wanted him. He told me I was a leech, hanging on to get whatever I could get.

Steve was like a derailed train moving at an unstoppable speed. Before I knew it, he had had his first baby outside of our marriage. The mother was one of his one-night stands. When she found out he was an NFL player, she jumped into bed with my husband three hours after meeting him. Two months later, before I had come to terms with the first baby, another woman called to tell us she was pregnant with his child.

Besides dealing with the betrayal and embarrassment I felt, I had to deal with the second woman's threats to go to the media. She wanted a check to keep her quiet, and a big one—big enough to threaten my family's financial livelihood. This woman was also a skillful stalker, and I couldn't believe that Steve had put our family in harm's way all for the sake of lying down with this lunatic.

At this point, Steve had a total of four children, our two and the two outside our marriage. I was beyond embarrassment. I felt powerless and was pregnant a third time, furiously trying to figure out how I could make it on my own with three kids. I had put away some money and thought I might buy a McDonald's franchise. That private dream got shattered when the judge ruled in the second mother's favor. An annuity had to be set up for her child. Since I was Steve's wife, my assets were not insulated from his and were needed to cover the annuity. My financial world crumbled, and under the circumstances I did not feel that I could make it on my own with two kids and a third on the way.

Our third baby was born, but Steve continued to demolish our lives. The negative publicity could not be contained. He was accused of driving under the influence and using recreational drugs, faced repeated charges of domestic violence, and continued to engage in extramarital affairs. Tired of doing damage control, his team cut him loose with a simple phone call. All his fame and fortune were gone after a two-minute, one-way conversation.

Despite his fall from grace, Steve still appeared to have no interest in me or in our children. There was nothing for me to hold on to. When we finally split up, I was lucky to get out with $30 and the three children in tow. I had to send the kids to my parents because I had no means of supporting them, and our house was in foreclosure. I stayed with a friend for some time, and my mother had to buy me a used car so I could get around.

At least I wouldn't be thrown outside naked in the snow, or shoved into an aquarium anymore. All I ever wanted was a husband who loved me and loved our children, but living in the spotlight with this wide receiver came at a very high price—and almost cost me my life.

Current Snapshot

Two of my children are honor students in college. I have plenty of suitors, but I am not thinking about remarriage right now. My mission is to coach my children into their full potential. I still have financial challenges, but I am dealing with them on my own terms. Admittedly, I had been spoiled. I still love beautiful clothes, but now I have found the magic of designer resale boutiques. In addition to my part-time job, I run a day spa, which has always been a dream of mine. My clients include the wives of professional athletes who can afford my fees. But I understand the trauma of being battered and neglected, and I frequently provide pro bono services to women who are traumatized or struggling like I once was. This is my way of encouraging other women to hang on to hope and go after their dreams.

Pearls of Wisdom......

From "Beware, Some Dreams Do Come True"

- Mothers do not always know best, especially when they are desperate to see their children live better lives than they have. Always listen to your own heart above the urgings of others.

- If you don't value your own life, no one else will.
- No fortune or fame is worth being treated as less than human—ever.
- If your spouse has one child outside of your marriage, heed the warning. A second child born out of wedlock is a sign for "game over."

BROKEN HONOR: BETH
Cause of Death: Emotional Disorder and Substance Abuse

I was from a very traditional yet open-minded Jewish family. Paul's family had emigrated from China. Still, Paul and I had plenty in common. We went to the same college and came from similar lifestyles. Our fathers were both entrepreneurs: mine owned a flower shop and his a Chinese restaurant. Neither of us was a stranger to hard work.

After dating for about three years, Paul asked me to marry him. We were still in school, but almost all of his fraternity brothers were engaged or married, and he wanted to follow suit. Paul had always tried to downplay his traditional Chinese upbringing and worked very hard to fit in. Most of my friends were getting the "Mrs." degree as well, so I accepted right away. Paul's mother was furious when we married—I was not Chinese.

I moved through college quickly, finishing my first degree in three years. It took Paul six and a half years to complete his bachelor's degree, even though he was brilliant. I went on to pursue two master's degrees, one in social work and the second in education. The social work degree would later prove to be invaluable to me.

Almost as soon as we were married, the problems started. I realized that Paul had anger management issues I had never witnessed while we were dating. It quickly became apparent that something very dark was pinned up inside of him, evidenced by his lack of interest in intimacy. In five years of marriage, we only had sex a couple of times—just enough to conceive our daughter, Amy.

I blamed myself and tried to perfect everything about my body. I told myself that if I lost weight, he might want me again. I changed my hairstyle half a dozen times and bought a new wardrobe. He never even noticed. I lived in a world of imaginary sex where I fantasized his obsession with my body.

Meanwhile, Paul forged a very successful career as a software engineer. He started spending nights at work. Insecure and suspicious from sex deprivation, I checked out his alibi by asking other women who had husbands in similar positions if their husbands worked nights. They told me it was quite plausible that he would occasionally have to pull all-nighters. Still, I suspected that it was more than software programming that was keeping him out all night. The day that our daughter was born, instead of spending the first night with us at the hospital, he left in a rush; he did not want to miss his bowling league. When I mentioned to him that I felt neglected, Paul told me I was paranoid and needed counseling. I was so depressed at that point that I was willing to try anything. So off to the counselor I went.

On our fifth wedding anniversary, he gave me an expensive watch. I told him that I appreciated the lovely gift, but I could not read the tiny numbers on the dial. He pulled out the receipt and told me to return it and get what I wanted. When I took it back, the jeweler asked me if I wanted to return any of the other items on the receipt. I hadn't even noticed that other pieces of jewelry were listed.

When I got home and looked around, I found other telling signs including multiple receipts from the same strip club. Paul was ruining our credit by taking out loans to support a secret lifestyle that, according to my findings that day, included lots of alcohol, drugs, and strippers. Now there was no denying the flashing red light.

He came home around four o'clock in the morning and lay down on the couch. I was still awake and heard the phone ring shortly after he arrived. After he took the call, he passed out. I grabbed his cell phone and looked for the last number dialed. It was for someone named Mary. I called it and she answered, but refused to give up any information when she heard my voice.

When he got up to go to work later that morning, I told him, "I know."

"You know what?" he mumbled, barely awake.

Not wanting to wake our sleeping baby, I asked him to come home for lunch that day so we could talk. He was visibly shaking as he hurried out the door, but did as I requested. When he came back that day, I told him, "You have a choice: you can get rid of her, or you can leave."

I guess he couldn't live without her, because he left that day, walking away from the baby and me as if we were an inconvenient nuisance. After a few months of separation, I finally talked him into agreeing to attend a joint counseling session. At the session, he said he wanted to work on the marriage but had no intention of removing Mary the stripper or the drugs from his life. The counselor gave me a look as if to say, "You know what you need to do."

The session confirmed the obvious: Paul had a severe bipolar disorder and was also abusing alcohol and drugs. He didn't want me sexually because he was getting his needs met outside the marriage. The marriage was beyond repair. The counselor told me in front of Paul that I needed to get out of the marriage. I went home that day and called an attorney.

The next day, out of respect, I called his parents and asked them to come over. Finally, I shared with them what I had endured throughout my marriage to their son. Trying to be tactful, I prefaced my story with the fact that he had been diagnosed with bipolar disorder. I gave them a folder that was filled with information on resources and support groups. Then I gave them another large envelope filled with all of the credit card bills and loan statements, proof of all the money he had spent to maintain the affair with Mary and his drug habit. Lastly, I informed them that he had left me and the baby to go be with a stripper.

His mother looked at me and asked in broken English, "Is she at least Chinese?" I couldn't even get angry about her blatant racism. It became obvious that Paul's emotional issues had their roots in his upbringing and dysfunctional family. I only wish I had taken the time to get to know his family and his background better before we married.

His parents left our home that day and never came back, coldly ignoring their baby granddaughter as if she had never been born. In their mind she didn't exist because, from that day forward, neither did their son. They disowned him entirely, and offered me no apologies, no explanations, no compassion, and no assistance.

We were soon divorced. There was nothing left to discuss. I think he must have been too high to read the fine print on the papers I served him with. I got everything that I requested from the divorce, including absolution from his debt.

Current Snapshot

About a year after the divorce, I met my true soul mate. We are now married, and he has become a father to my little girl. We have moved to the West Coast and are expecting our first baby together. My husband makes enough money as a publisher to allow me to stay home with the kids. He is also Jewish and shares my values and religious beliefs. I am finally content, married to a man who, like my father and brothers, loves his wife unconditionally.

Pearls of Wisdom.....

From "Broken Honor"

- Marriage is not a fashion accessory. Don't get married because it's trendy or because it's what everyone else is doing.
- Get to know your prospective in-laws. Your husband's relationship with them speaks volumes about what you can expect from the marriage.
- The first sign of an emotional disorder needs to be addressed professionally. If your mate refuses treatment or counseling, you need to leave.

PEACE AND RELEASE: LACEY
Cause of Death: Drug Addiction

On our wedding night, my new husband, Bentley, went into the bathroom and came back with a little square package full of white powder. He asked me if I wanted to try some.

"You just sniff a little up your nose, and you're in heaven," he said.

"I don't think so," I replied. "I'm not putting anything up my nose, and neither should you."

Little did I know that this white powder would soon become my worst enemy—it was his mistress and my hell on earth. Barely two weeks into our marriage, he didn't come home from work one night and never called. When I couldn't track him down, I started calling the hospitals, jails, and morgues. He strolled in casually around 2:00 a.m. and gave me some crazy excuse about going over to a coworker's house and losing track of time.

After seven years of marriage, I decided one day that I couldn't live with an addict any longer. Nor could I afford to jeopardize the safety and well-being of our three small children. I came to this conclusion as I was driving home from work, but once home, I sat paralyzed in the garage. I didn't know how I could gather the courage to do what I knew needed to be done.

After I prayed in the car for about twenty minutes, the answer came to me: if I walked into the house and he was high, I would tell him he had to leave. I slowly got out of the car and walked inside. I kissed my kids and asked the nanny to take them out for a very long walk. I slowly strolled into the den, where he lay on the sofa watching television as usual. I greeted him, but he didn't look up or respond. I knew the signs.

I sat in a chair next to the sofa, and I asked him to look me in the eye, which he couldn't. I knew then without hesitation that he was using again. Determined to keep the promise I had just made to God and myself, I said to him in a gentle and steady voice, "You have to go."

"What did you say?" he said.

I slowly repeated my words. "You have to go, now."

He laughed nervously and said, "OK! Whatever."

"You need to listen to me," I said, keeping my voice calm. "It's not like all the other times. You cannot sweet-talk your way out of this. You have to go. You can pack a few things now and make arrangements to get the rest of your stuff later."

I went into the bedroom, picked up the phone, and called my father. He lived about ten minutes away. I simply asked him to come over immediately. Then I dialed 911 and said, "My husband needs to leave my house immediately, and I sense there may be some trouble. Can you please send a car?" My father arrived before the police. I had put some of Bentley's things in a duffel bag while I waited. I handed the bag off to my dad when he arrived. I told my father that I would give him the details later, but that Bentley had to go. Dad threw the bag at him and told him to leave. The arrival of the police confirmed there would be no scene.

Bentley left. The man I married, the father of my three children, the corporate executive with the devil on his back, was out of my house. Release had finally come, but it was only the beginning of a long journey to find peace. I had been in denial for too long as I witnessed at close range some of Bentley's drug-induced antics, including:

- His arrest for possession after running a red light
- His physical abuse of me, including grabbing me by the neck when I was eight months pregnant
- His failure to pick our son up from daycare because he was too high to remember
- His letting our homeowner's insurance lapse for eight months. I only found out when we were denied our claim for hurricane damage to the roof
- The loss of his career and destruction of our finances
- His probation officer showing up on the doorstep during a birthday party for my eighty-five-year-old grandmother
- His inability to stay clean for more than a week after very costly drug rehab

My parents had long sensed that things weren't great, but they didn't really know the half of it. My pride wouldn't allow me to admit I had made a colossal mistake. I was a college graduate. I had earned my master's degree in one year. I was smarter than the rest of the world, or so I thought. How could I have married someone so screwed up? I was embarrassed for both of us.

Within a year, my divorce was final. In the divorce settlement, I agreed to accept half of what he should have paid me. I would have gladly paid that much and more for peace of mind and freedom from Bentley. He was still angry with me, and made several threats to kill me. I moved four times in three years. Each time, he would hire someone to find me, and I would have to move again. My father even temporarily moved in with me, sleeping on the sofa with a gun beside him when the threats were at their worst. It was almost four years before I felt comfortable being alone, but eventually we got past the threats.

I was fortunate to have had the support of my family throughout this time. Even though they were in the dark about the situation for many years, when the light finally came on, they came to my rescue. Until their deaths, my parents helped me raise my kids. I also had the support of wonderful friends who never judged me, and supported me both emotionally and spiritually.

I thought I was free when I left the courthouse with my divorce papers. The truth is, I wasn't really released until about ten years later when I forgave him and let go of the painful memories. The healing process from emotional abuse is often longer than that of physical abuse. It is much harder to walk away from a relationship than it is to enter one, because of the emotional investment involved. I knew God would guide me out of this terrible situation. All I had to do was take the first step.

Current Snapshot

It has now been almost twenty years since the divorce. Bentley ended up living in his father's basement, and his drug use continued for many more years. During this time he was in and out of menial jobs and rehab programs. He claims to be clean today and works at the airport as a skycap, carrying people's luggage.

Bentley and I don't talk often, but when we do the conversation is civil. I pray for him. I have no love for him, but he is the father of my children and a child of God no matter what. No one is perfect, and none of us knows where our journey will lead.

I feel blessed today because I am finally able to live freely and fulfill my own purposes. I have a wonderful job where I feel I am making a difference. I am writing and painting again, pursuits that I had lost sight of in the fire of my marriage. My children are doing well, and I am at peace with the world.

Pearls of Wisdom.....

From "Peace and Release"

- The vows may say "for better or for worse," but that does not mean that you should endanger your life and the lives of your children for the sake of staying married.
- Living with a drug addict is very dangerous. If you find yourself in such a situation, do not keep this dark secret to yourself. Your family and friends are there to help you. Find a way to communicate your situation to someone you trust.
- Listen to your spirit, that inner voice deep inside of you. That is your direct connection to God and your instinctual protection.

- Whenever you find yourself in an uncomfortable situation, leave. If it doesn't feel right, chances are it isn't.

Coroner's Report on Secrets, Lies, and Addictions

Sheila Peters, PhD, Licensed Psychologist, Associate Professor of Psychology at Fisk University, on Substance Abuse in Marital Relationships

In the early stages of relationship building, many people miss or choose to ignore obvious signs that their partner is at risk for alcoholism or drug addiction. We do this not because we are weak or easily deceived, but because we often go into relationships searching only for love and happiness. But substance abuse usually causes a relationship to be riddled with deception and conflict. Even if it existed prior to the relationship, substance abuse can also be an excuse for avoiding and denying the existence of other relationship problems.

Because potential partners often meet in social settings in which alcohol or other drugs are used as a means of relaxation or celebration, people may use the substance to present an incomplete representation of themselves. They may also rely on it to cope with excitement and uncertainty during the early stages of the relationship. Furthermore, substance abuse often serves as a means by which to deflect, ignore, or excuse painful feelings or behavior, allowing the perpetrator to avoid responsibility. The substance may be a scapegoat, but the issues always run deeper.

For men, substance abuse is often identified as the primary issue, but it is possible that the abuse masks other emotional challenges such as depression and anxiety, which are often underdiagnosed in men. Men experience significant feelings of loss, betrayal, and hurt, just as women do. Unfortunately, men are not generally encouraged to talk about their feelings or cultivate their emotional intelligence. Even for the most articulate of men, it is often difficult to express their feelings about marriage or relationships.

As a relationship unravels, substance abuse provides an unhealthy platform for expression, which often takes the form of hateful language and disrespectful behavior. As a man experiences the loss of control that accompanies the demise of a relationship, his use of a substance such as drugs or alcohol is likely to increase. This behavior is an attempt to self-medicate, to deal with difficult feelings, but ultimately it only contributes to the mounting problems in the relationship.

In already troubled relationships, substance abuse always complicates things. Individuals who previously struggled with the overuse of a substance are at increased risk for chronic abuse if their relationship is floundering or reaches an emotional roadblock. The possibility of a divorce or breakup is troubling to both husbands and wives, especially as it is often viewed as a personal failure by family, friends, and society. Drugs and alcohol are often used or abused at this juncture to dull the pain, but again serve to exacerbate the situation.

The effects of a partner's substance abuse go far beyond the immediate relationship. If children are involved, they are prone to learn to exist in deception and have difficulty confronting relationship challenges. Many wives tend to regard it as their personal responsibility to help and heal an addicted husband, failing to realize or acknowledge that professionals are far better equipped to help him battle his demons. Both partners risk falling into similar dysfunctional patterns in future relationships, especially if they have failed to acknowledge and deal with the issues that lie beneath or go beyond the abuse of drugs and alcohol. It is important for anyone affected by substance abuse—whether directly or indirectly, through their own use or through that of a loved one—to work through all levels of the struggle and learn to properly contextualize the issues in order to build a framework for a healthy future.

Interlude

Reclaiming Your Joy

The walls around me have come down. I have been set free from the prison of our marriage, and my new life is about to begin. As my eyes readjust to the light I went so long without, I can see that our failed marriage was a necessary lesson that taught me to value my life. When I look at you now, I feel no anger or urge to retaliate. In letting go of the past, I am drained of all its poison. I am a clean and empty vessel ready to be filled with new hope and joy. I feel nothing but a burning desire to be fully alive and let you go.

Journal excerpt from D. L. Mars

In Part I, we witnessed scores of women who sought love and instead endured immense heartbreak and disappointment. Each woman's situation caused her great pain and pushed her to the brink of despair. The selection of stories provided a survey of some of the most common warning signs and symptoms that indicate a marriage is headed for the graveyard.

No one said marriage would be easy. Even the happiest of married couples will admit to traveling on some rough roads. This rocky terrain is a part of life, but tough times should not be synonymous with calling it quits. The key is to travel these roads hand in hand with your partner, supporting each other whenever the going is hard. Marriages that manage this successfully—marriages that are based on mutual respect and shared values—will endure the test of time in spite of the direst circumstances. Marriages that never achieve this common ground, however, will always struggle and often fail.

Part II of this book looks beyond the causes of marital demise and focuses on the stories of women who permanently reclaimed their lives by setting new norms. The women directly address what it means to take responsibility for their own happiness and embrace the power of living with purpose.

We all have a natural tendency to hold on to the past. Even a terminal relationship can project the illusion of security because its symptoms are predictable. A luxurious lifestyle can make one think twice about leaving an unhealthy relationship. But life offers daily blessings and opportunities to grow into your luscious destiny. If you can release the past, you open yourself up to a bright future full of surprises and new beginnings.

The first step to moving on is learning to forgive, and you must start by forgiving yourself. We all fall short of expectations sometimes. Making errors in judgment is a part of life. If you have lived to talk about perils, then you have survived the worst and are on your way to victory!

Almost ten years after my divorce, I finally decided that I loved myself more than I despised my ex-husband. It wasn't until then that my life started coming back together. I used to get upset about the ways in which I felt he was neglecting our children, but finally I realized that it was his loss that he had not spent quality time with them. I prayed that he would develop a burning desire to get to know and love them unconditionally as a father should, and God answered my prayer.

He and I have settled into an amicable relationship that works for both of us. Would it bother me if he remarried? Only if his new wife were unkind to my children. In hindsight I cannot believe I allowed myself to experience so much grief before I allowed myself to reclaim joy.

It takes a lot of energy to be angry. Anger causes both physical and mental stress, which can be deadly. At the very least it will hold you in emotional bondage. You must learn to forgive and get on with the privilege of living.

I know what your objections are to this oversimplified illustration. Your husband was a liar and adulterer. He abandoned your family, or stole money from you. Perhaps he even physically abused you. Whatever it was, you have to let it go. You don't have to be on the receiving end of his abusive behavior anymore. Step aside, release him, and rejoice, knowing that his internal war is no longer your battle. That simple fact in itself is worth celebrating.

Force yourself to pack up your heartache, disappointments, and betrayal along with the old family portraits and scrapbooks. Put them where they belong, on a shelf in a closet. You may want to leave pictures of him in your children's rooms, but you are in no way obligated to build a shrine of memories to him. If there are some traditions that you observed as a family and you find it too painful to continue them, develop new ones.

Do not dwell on your past lifestyle, especially if it was affluent. Remember the old saying, "The best things in life are not things." Fight for what is rightfully yours, but keep materialistic concerns in perspective. As you move forward, do not prejudge potential suitors based on how you were treated in the past. A negative and defeatist attitude can sabotage a new relationship before it has the chance to fully materialize.

Divorce is a death. It is imperative that you take the time to adequately reflect upon and mourn your loss. First, be still. Then pray. Cry it out. Take personal inventory by keeping a journal. Focus on your physical, mental, and financial health, and seek professional counseling if needed. Then assess, adjust, and progress toward your road to happier days. It is impossible to begin to feel alive again unless you can learn to leave the past where it belongs. Imagine two forces pulling you simultaneously. The future is beckoning you to move forward toward the light—to new energy, new opportunities, and new blessings. The past is tugging you back toward the darkness, reminding you of the horrific things that have happened, daring you to get even. Stay focused, and don't allow yourself to be confused or deceived. Leaving the past behind does not mean that you forget what has happened to you. On the contrary, everything that you experience—whether good or bad—should provide a lesson in living. These lessons build up your character, offer invaluable insight into what makes you who you are, and make you stronger and wiser.

Embrace the necessary lessons from the past, open the door to a season of new beginnings, and get ready to live happier than ever after the divorce.

*To everything there is a season
a time for every purpose under heaven . . .
a time to plant,
and a time to pluck what is planted . . .
a time to break down,
and a time to build up;
a time to weep,
and a time to laugh.*
—*Ecclesiastes 3:1-4*

Making of a Warrior

With my big sister Jackye and big brother Quentin Jr. (Brother).

The calm before the storm.

My brother and his girlfriend Peggy posing with his car just days before his death.

At my debutante ball I would have given up my Queen's Crown to have my brother back.

My room during senior year of High School. Can you dig it?!

AKA portrait at USC
(Iota Beta Chapter)

Pregnancy should be filled with pride and joy, mine was filled with shame and anguish.

From the time he was born Alex has been my change agent.

Celebrating with Executive Team after Frito-Lay wins coveted NMSDC Corporation of the Year.
This was my first time riding in the corporate jet!

Beware of the Fairy Tale

Embrace the wisdom of the inner child.

I should have listened to the inner child... I was caught up in the Fairy Tale!

In my expansive showroom. The plan was to retire by 40. Oh well!

We never moved into my dream home.

It was painful pulling the family portraits off the wall.

Little Debbie always told it like it was.

Debra's Battle Field

I soon learned single parenting was no fairy tale.

Within 6 months I mourned the death of my marriage and my beloved father.

The outside world thought my life was privileged. I mastered the art of faking happiness.

My lowest point… I ate my feelings and stopped looking in the mirror.

"A girl's gotta do what a girl's gotta do!"

Last Christmas in Dallas:
Touchdown!

And She Lived Happier Ever After...

I left a legacy on Legacy Dr.

My first Thanksgiving home (2015) in
Los Angeles surrounded by family.

My first Mother's Day home at
the beach with my crown jewels.

My Godmother stuck by me
every step of the journey.

Dear Stress… Let's break Up!

...He'll be here in a minute

PART II

The Happier Ever After
Lives in You

Accept Reality

While I have developed an attachment to all of the women who appear in this book, Marvella from "The Wrong Girl" is probably the one I admire the most. Beyond her sassiness and what some might judge as "rough edges" is a woman from whom we can all learn a critical lesson. No material thing or false security blanket is worth pawning your dignity for.

Most women can appreciate the benefits of having a constant companion, a second income, a built-in handyman, a bedtime buddy, and someone to help with the kids. But Marvella found the strength to fast-forward past the nightmare on the horizon and see the big picture—Swabena had long-term plans that didn't include her. Just like any other woman, she wanted to live in the "happily ever after," but she did not make excuses for his derisive behavior. When she discovered the truth—that she was being used for a green card—she took action and sought the happier ever after life without Swabena. She loved herself and her children enough to escape from his drumbeat of deceit that would have left her vulnerable from every imaginable perspective.

Swabena's plan to leave Marvella for his African wife was not something that could have been remedied in marriage counseling. So why hang around and watch the drama play out? Unlike Cinderella, she knew there was no "fairy godmother" coming to rescue her. Here's the part I especially love: she summoned up the discipline to keep her mouth shut while she developed a plan to sabotage his immigration fraud. She determined when it was time to call the big orange pumpkin to come carry her and her children away. She went from being a ball of confusion to having a ball! Off they rode to celebrate the power of self-love. You gotta love it!

How many times have you stumbled upon an ugly truth and instead of confronting and resolving the matter, you internalized it to the point that you became depressed or physically ill? Discovering that your husband has been snorting away the mortgage payment or having an affair with his assistant is enough to make any God-fearing woman think unchristian thoughts. Learn the difference between a human slipup—like failing to pay a bill on time—and an overt character flaw—like stealing money from the family savings account—and take action accordingly.

I once attended a women's Friday evening fellowship that made me want to run out of the room screaming in disgust. A woman shared her story, telling how her husband had left her three years prior for another woman. He also made it very clear that he did not love her anymore and wanted a divorce.

To the discerning woman, this would have been a sign to shut down shop. Sadly, she was still hoping he would return and repopulate her fairy tale. The thought of her wasting her life hoping he will return is very disturbing. It would have been inappropriate for me to confront this stranger regarding her heartfelt testimony. But before I left, I whispered to the organizer to please get her into counseling as soon as possible.

If someone tells you or shows you he doesn't want to be married to you anymore, believe him. Find the inner strength to let your heart see what your eyes refuse to. It takes maturity to see a bad situation for what it really is. It takes faith to know that happiness awaits you elsewhere. It takes fortitude to walk away from disappointment. It takes courage to find the blessing that is buried in loss.

I encourage you to look at your own situation and determine if you are being real about your circumstances, or if you have fallen into a pit of delusion like the woman from the Friday night gathering. We all know God frowns upon divorce; however, consider viewing God from a more contemporary perspective. He is not mysterious but deliberate. Nor does he enjoy watching his children suffer for lack of wisdom. Stay alert, and keep your eyes and ears open for whatever clarifying information he will allow you to have access to.

Franklin D. Roosevelt once said, "Repetition does not transform a lie into the truth." Don't allow anyone, not even yourself, to feed you lies that can gravely impact your life. No matter how much it hurts, when you embrace truth you will be freed from having to live with or perpetuate a secret.

As women, we must not isolate one another because of differing beliefs, zip codes, bank accounts, or skin color. We must support one another and learn to embrace and celebrate truth even if it initially is bitter tasting. When you accept reality you release your spirit to soar. Mary Poppins was right: a spoonful of sugar does make the medicine go down. Focus on the sweet possibilities of life beyond deceit and move forward. Open wide . . .

The "A" List: Alison

Patrick and I felt an instant connection when we met while serving jury duty. He was one of the most gorgeous men I had ever seen. His hazel eyes were penetrating and made the hair on the back of my neck stand up. We decided to marry after dating for eight months. We reasoned that since we were both over forty, it shouldn't take forever to figure out if we were compatible.

About six months into the marriage, Patrick came home and announced he wanted to take me to an A-list Hollywood party. I was excited but curious as to how we had received an invitation to a party in Bel Air. Patrick dismissed my skepticism and told me to put on something sexy. Still a newlywed, I thought, "Great, my husband wants to show me off!" I took extra care putting on my makeup and getting dressed.

As we snaked up the steep hill on Mulholland Drive, my eyes couldn't believe what they saw. We were in front of one of the most beautiful mansions I had ever seen. Once inside, I was surprised that so many people seemed to know Patrick. I wondered why he had never mentioned this set of friends before. I also wondered how a baggage inspector had gained entry into this circle of the rich and the famous.

Feeling invisible and out of place, I took myself on an unguided tour of the mansion. I proceeded down a seemingly endless hallway and counted eight bedrooms, four on each side. As my eyes adjusted to the dim light, I noticed decorative dispensers mounted on the wall. They were filled with sanitizers, towels, and, most strangely of all, condoms. Then I heard a mixture of groans, moans, laughter, and music coming out of one of the bedrooms. Since the doors were open, I peeked inside. I had stumbled upon an orgy. I was both offended and curious at the same time.

I rushed to find Patrick, wanting to tell him I was ready to go home. As I approached him, another woman came out of nowhere and lifted up her dress, exposing her nakedness, and began to gyrate against his thigh. My intuition kicked into overdrive. These people were not strangers to Patrick.

I grabbed his arm to signal that I wanted to leave. He yanked away from me and made it very clear that he did not want to go. I was too uptight, he told me, and needed to loosen up. I was stunned. Why would I want to share my husband with anyone? Through clenched teeth, Patrick explained that swinging would spice up our sex life and that we were lucky to be invited to this party. He told me that this was an exclusive crowd, and to stay on the list you not only had to bring a partner but offer them as a participant in the "fun."

I didn't give a hoot about these people or their overcharged libidos. I wanted to get as far away from this them as fast as I could. That night was the first nail in the coffin of our marriage. What had I done to make him think that I was interested in swinging? My husband, who had promised to honor and protect me, had planned to use me as a bargaining chip for a night of fantasy. I felt dirty, betrayed, and devalued.

One Saturday morning a few weeks later, Patrick mentioned another invitation, this time to a barbeque. I figured if we were going to stay married, I would give him a second chance, and a barbeque seemed harmless. I agreed to go. I focused on the beautiful weather and smooth jazz. I did not allow myself to dwell on the Bel Air incident.

Once in Orange County, we pulled up to a perfectly ordinary-looking stucco house, a typical single-family California home. It struck me as odd that there were no other cars present when we arrived two hours after the party was supposed to start. It turned out that it was the home of couple about the same age as Patrick and me. Soon after we arrived, the guys went outside to smoke cigars and drink beer. Once again, I found myself feeling out of place. Patrick had left me alone to make small talk with a total stranger. Susan, the hostess, led me into their game room where we settled on the couch to visit over our glasses of iced tea.

She leaned toward me as she said, "So you're Elena, right?" I wondered how she knew my middle name, as that was not information I normally shared. Before I could answer her, she lunged toward me, slipped her hand inside my blouse, and started fondling my left breast.

I jumped up and screamed, "Get off me! What do you think you are doing?"

Susan looked at me like I was crazy and asked why I was suddenly playing games. "Patrick said you were dying to hook up with me. You sent me all those naughty emails, and you're the one who suggested that we finally get together."

When she realized how startled I was by her words and actions, her face became flushed. Her next words were slow and deliberate. "Are you telling me that you were not the one who sent me all those hot emails?"

My husband had once again offered me up like a sacrificial lamb. He had begged me on our honeymoon to pose for the provocative pictures he had emailed to this stranger. They had been meant for his eyes only. Susan apologized profusely and told me that she never would have approached me if she had known the emails were not from me. I believed her, but I still had to deal with Patrick.

I ran outside and told him we were leaving immediately. Patrick followed me out the door and got into the car without protest. The drive back to Los Angeles seemed to last for an eternity. I screamed, yelled, and punched him in the arm. He never uttered a word. I was determined that I wouldn't be taken in a third time.

A few days later, he told me that he had to attend a business meeting in Las Vegas. I could not imagine what kind of business meeting a nonsupervisory TSA agent would have in Las Vegas. As soon as he pulled out of the driveway, I called my cousin, Claire, who worked at a major casino in Las Vegas. I told her about Patrick's pornographic and demented mindset and asked for her help.

Before he had even arrived in the city, Claire had hired a local private investigator to follow him. He was so caught up in his tryst that he never suspected he was under surveillance. For three days, the PI followed Patrick and his constant companions (a young woman, probably a teenager, and a man who appeared to be in his late sixties). The threesome spent the majority of their time in a room with one king-size bed, according to investigator. Moans, groans, and laughter were heard day and night. By the time Patrick arrived back at our house, I had changed the locks and tossed his clothes out into the yard. As a final touch, I pinned a note on top of the pile that read: Stay out of my life. Your ex-wife.

I had let my loneliness cloud my thinking to the point that I married a man I hardly knew. His outer appearance drew me in, but he was rotten to the core, an immoral opportunist with an insatiable appetite for kinky sex. Luckily, Patrick's sordid lifestyle caused me to snap back to reality while my health and sanity were still intact. I divorced him, relocated east, completed nursing school, and started a new life free of swinging and lies.

KEEP YOUR OPTIONS OPEN: LANEY

Our youngest daughter, Lacey, made the call. As she sat at the bottom of the staircase and watched her father being taken to the waiting police car, I knew that a part of her was dying. I knew the madness had to stop—if for no other reason than to protect Lacey's childhood. I could not allow her to witness violence in our home ever again. As her mother, I was responsible for protecting her, but that night my daughter was protecting me. She intuitively knew that if she did not call for help, I could have died at the hands of her father. My husband, Lance, the community leader, entrepreneur, and power broker, was also a batterer.

Unless God changed him completely, I would never again allow Lance back into my life. The stakes were too high. I had suffered from physical, emotional, and financial abuse during our marriage. I repeatedly asked God to change him. Instead, God spoke to my spirit, telling me I needed to change.

After Lance moved out, he made it his mission to make my life miserable. His most obvious play for power was to move our money around faster than a squirrel gathers nuts. At that moment, I had no choice but to let go of things and hope for the best. During the divorce proceedings, Lance's strategy was intimidation. He lied and did everything in his power to block me from gaining access to our assets.

When the minutes of one particular proceeding were read at a follow-up meeting, it appeared to me that his know-it-all attorney had made an error. My first instinct was to correct him. Lance had not agreed to the point referenced. I tried to speak, but no words escaped my mouth. As a result of the lawyer's error, the judge ruled in my favor. I trembled all the way to the car, fully aware that God had come to my rescue.

The more I trusted God, the more he rewarded me. One day as I prayed, I realized that I was still unable to recover from the toxicity of the marriage because I had not yet forgiven Lance. That weekend, when I dropped off Lacey for visitation, I found myself standing in Lance's foyer apologizing to him! Instead of offering forgiveness to him, I was delivering the script that God had given me.

"Lance, I apologize for not standing up to you when I should have, and for speaking when I should have acquiesced when I was your wife." As my lips formed the words, I knew that God was speaking through me. As crazy as it might sound, I left Lance's home that day feeling as if I had just been released from prison. The door to peace had been flung open.

When I remember our daughter sitting there on the stairs with a look of horror and fear on her eyes, everything else is irrelevant. I am so blessed that I have the flexibility today to spend time with Lacey. Now that things have settled down, I have plenty of options, both professionally and socially. I attend social events when I feel like it, sometimes with an escort, sometimes alone. Rather than attending every gala and black-tie affair, however, I also invest my time mentoring children and delivering meals to the elderly. In lieu of hosting fancy dinner parties, I have a few close friends over for a pajama party. Rather than surround myself with pretentious and pompous opportunists, I enjoy the company of friends and loved ones.

I continue to let God lead every step of my journey. By obeying him, I have developed a wonderful friendship with Lance that is filled with mutual respect and a genuine admiration. We are both committed to being excellent parents to Lacey. We have regular family meetings and discuss her social calendar, college plans, challenges, and life plan. On occasions, we attend family gatherings with our significant others. I guess we are truly one big happy family. I see God working in each of our lives.

Two Queens in the Castle: Faith

From the time I was eighteen years old, all I ever wanted was to be married. While other girls were applying to colleges and planning their careers, I fantasized about what to name my imaginary children.

Within a few months of meeting Jack, I thought my fairy tale had come true. I had no doubt he was the one. He was tall and handsome, and I could imagine how gorgeous our children would be. He was everything I had ever wanted in a husband: attentive, kind, and easy to get along with. Even our friends agreed that we looked like royalty.

We married when I was only twenty-one. When the FBI deployed him to an assignment in Minneapolis, I was thrilled. I felt important and empowered as the trophy wife of an FBI agent. After two years of marriage, I gave birth to our son, Charley. I was living my dream life.

I had every reason to believe that I was the apple of my husband's eye. He was considerate, loving, and very affectionate. He would even keep me company most days as I dressed and applied my makeup. He said that he loved looking at me.

As a fashion stylist, I have always been very meticulous. I believe there is a place for everything and everything belongs in its place. Whether I'm working on my closet or a client's, I set them all up as if they were boutiques.

One day, I was in my closet arranging my shoes when I noticed an unfamiliar box on the top shelf. I thought maybe Jack was hiding a gift for me. As I attempted to pull the box down, it fell to the floor and the contents scattered. There were pictures everywhere. As I picked some of them up, my chest tightened. I saw images of a woman standing in our house and wearing a dress just like one of mine, but the woman in the picture wasn't me. A terrible thought occurred to me. I can't believe Jack has had some woman in my home dressing up in my clothes! My Prince Charming was a frog.

As I examined the pictures more closely, my heart stopped beating. I realized that the "woman" in the pictures was Jack! There was no denying it. What kind of sick joke was this? I paced the room, vacillating between emotions, feeling shock, anger, sadness, and confusion. I could not summon up any plausible explanations as to why my Jack, the man of my dreams, was dressed as a woman. I prayed it was something job-related, but deep down inside I knew better. I felt as if someone had stabbed me in my gut.

Jack had recently become more withdrawn and distant. Prior to my discovery, I sensed something was wrong, but I just couldn't put my finger on it. Now my head would not stop spinning. As I waited for Jack to come home, I contemplated what I would say to him. This situation was so surreal that I couldn't talk to anyone other than him about it, not even my mother.

It seemed like an eternity passed before he came home from work that evening. As soon as we were alone in the room, I threw the pictures on the coffee table. "What is this, what is this, what is this?" I kept asking. "Please, help me understand why you were dressed up like a woman. Was it for one of your a top-secret assignments? I know, it's April Fool's Day. Is this a practical joke?" He looked at me and let out a long sigh, as if relieved. "There were so many times that I wanted to tell you about this," he said.

My heart almost pounded out of its chest cavity as I prayed, "God, please no!" After a few minutes, reality started to set in. FBI agents were shrewd. It was not happenstance that I found those pictures in the closet. Apparently, he had planted the box there hoping I would find it one day and put him out of his misery.

Jack admitted that he enjoyed dressing like a woman—falsies and all. I thought back to all the times he had watched me in the mirror in the bathroom as I put on makeup and selected outfits. He was getting tips! Jack told me that for a long time he had wished he had been born a girl, that he felt he was born into the wrong body. He had been dressing in women's clothing for years, even during his previous marriage. He said he was tired of living a lie and no longer wanted to live his life as a man. He was grateful that I had figured out on my own what he had been searching for the strength to tell me. He actually hoped that I would understand and that we could remain married. Most importantly he wanted us to remain friends. He continued to tell me how much he loved me and how much he appreciated that I always had his back.

Before this revelation I had been contemplating leaving him because something told me that he had misrepresented his connection to God. My discovery that day was confirmation. The truth was that he hated the God I served, and this was enough to drive me away from the marriage. The more I processed our past life the angrier I became. By the time he went to bed I was filled with rage. This man was a fraud, and he had robbed me of my fairy tale. I could not begin to process what I would tell our son one day when he was old enough to understand. I told God I was going to kill Jack. I rushed to the bedroom where he was sleeping. The door was unlocked, but for whatever reason, I couldn't get in. I struggled with that door for over two hours before I gave up.

The next morning after he left for work, I ran through the house grabbing whatever I could fit into two bags, one for me and the other for Charley. I was suffocating inside the walls of lies he had erected in our house. I called my mother to tell her that her grandson and I were coming home and that I would explain later. I purchased two one-way tickets, first class because my nerves were shot to hell. That day I left behind a closetful of beautiful clothes, my marriage, and the ugly truth about Jack. I filed for divorce immediately. When a man no longer wants to be a man, all hope ceases. I knew that no counseling could fix a marriage that had been built on lies and an identity crisis.

I was very blessed to have God's hand on me during my last night with Jack. Had God not intervened I probably would have killed Jack that night, and our son would have lost both his father and his mother to a grave and a prison cell.

I was once asked if being married to "such a man" made me question my own femininity. My unequivocal answer remains no! If anything, it further validated my femininity. I do not take credit for my strength and beauty; God equipped me with these attributes. I am not a Bible-toting, preachy woman, but I am a woman who fears nothing but God, the only being able to love unconditionally. I knew that there was no reason to torture myself over my husband's internal war. All I could do was pray for his healing, even if that meant not being a part of his future.

Those were Jackye's demons, not mine. He had never healed from being molested as a young child; he had never forgiven God. Jack no longer works for the FBI. He is now "Jackye" and lives on the East Coast. He has had a sex change, but he still lives in a very dark place. Even though he looks different on the outside, nothing inside has changed. His soul is still tortured. To this day, Jackye is without peace. If anything, Jackye has probably learned that it is more difficult to live as a woman than as a man.

My healing came from James 1:1-12, especially the line, "Blessed is the man who endures temptation." Once our son was older, I carefully explained to him why his father and I broke up. I am now remarried and enjoy a full-time career as a celebrity stylist. I love my job and my new husband. What's more, I feel certain that I am married to a man who plans to stay one. As the book of James instructs, I have learned to "count it all joy."

If a man really cares for you, his actions will speak for him. Nothing is sweeter than knowing a man truly cherishes his special lady. When he does, he will do anything to keep her. Above all, he will let others know that she is his cherished life partner. When he wants you for his own, he makes it known to the world.

Do you really want someone in your life who does not treat you with respect and admiration? Will you seek and accept love under any circumstances? If you can't seem to tear yourself away from an unhealthy relationship, take comfort in knowing that people come into your life for a reason, for a season or, when destined, a lifetime. Even if you have done your premarital due diligence, your husband's temporary tenure might be beyond your control—just intended for a season instead of a lifetime, as you had originally hoped.

And you shall know the truth, and the truth shall make you free.
—John 8:32

New Beginnings

Starting over after heartbreak takes courage, especially if you are walking away from a substantial palace and a king's ransom. I have personally experienced this, and also witnessed and heard stories of other women who stayed in dead-end marriages because they didn't want to abandon the title, the diamond, or the stuff. Let's rewind to Deana from "In a Heartbeat." After escaping a long-standing abusive relationship, she lingered in a seven-year divorce proceeding in an attempt to hold on to her financial assets. It took having her chest cracked open and a quadruple bypass surgery for her to finally put the priceless value of her life into perspective. Once she adjusted her attitude and prepared to lose half of her queendom, in the end she won it all! She received a bucket of blessings, as evidenced by an exploding business, her dream home, a luxury car, and a doting soul mate to share it all with!

Bishop T. D. Jakes set the stage for embracing new beginnings when he said, "If you die over who you knew, you will miss who you are supposed to meet." That's another mantra I live by! When heartbreak strikes and bad news brews, we have to learn to trust God to work it out—even if that means starting again at the beginning and alone. A fresh start symbolizes an end to the pain of the past. A new beginning brings the promise of hope and reinvention.

You have to hold your ground and put your ego in check when you find your financial situation or social status has been turned upside down compliments of divorce. I know because I have been there. I have driven friends to the airport when they were on their way to the kind of luxury vacations I could no longer afford. I have shopped at Ross, T.J. Maxx, and Marshalls while my friends scooped up St. John Knits and David Yurman jewelry from Saks Fifth Avenue. I traded in my beloved Jaguar for a truck. And yes, I sold off the couture fashion from my closet and jewelry for pennies on the dollar. There's a lesson to be learned in this too. In the midst of my humility, I find peace knowing that I am living an authentic life free of the trauma that goes with being married to an imposter or having an imposter living inside of me.

Your new beginnings will be made to order. It could mean a new hobby, a new career, relocation, a new look, a different set of friends, and hopefully a healthier lifestyle. Whatever you do, do what you can, where you are, with what you have. God will honor that. Beautiful you are, but helplessness is an ugly trait. Don't be a sleeping beauty and wait for someone to wake you up from a nightmarish past with a "magic kiss." Wake up, get up, stay up on life, and walk boldly into your future!

Don't Count Me Out: Joan

My husband, Karl, didn't want a divorce. Why would he? For years, he had lived a glamorous life complete with a trophy wife and four well-behaved, smart, and attractive children. He kept his mistress within convenient reach, only forty miles away from his home base. Together, Karl and I amassed a substantial fortune from a variety of entrepreneurial ventures and real-estate investments. We belonged to the right circles, were members at the right country club, lived in the right neighborhood, and attended the right church. Karl was handsome, charming, and well respected in the community. By all outward appearances, he was any woman's dream.

He also had me right where he wanted me: financially dependent, emotionally needy, and accustomed to a privileged lifestyle. He grew very smug and assumed that I would never dare to rock the boat. For a long time, he was absolutely right. I wanted my husband and my family intact more than anything else. I loved coordinating our annual holiday portraits, going on our European family vacations, and traveling to our second home in Mexico.

When our last child departed for college, there were no other witnesses in the household, and Karl had no further incentive for good behavior. He constantly badgered me verbally. Suddenly our money was "his" money. He withheld funds from me and would dole out petty cash only when I begged. I had to ask him for cash before I could buy a loaf of bread.

After twenty-seven years of marriage, I was forced to accept the fact that our children had been the buffer in our relationship. In an attempt to salvage our marriage, I asked Karl if we could go to counseling. He refused point-blank. When I finally accepted that the marriage could not be saved, I tried to devise an exit strategy.

At the time, I wanted a master's degree more than anything else. I went back to school to study marriage, family, and child counseling. Karl paid for the first year to pacify me, but I had to suffer through all his snide remarks. He said that no one would hire me because I was too old, and he continued to berate me about everything.

I expedited my timeline. I decided that when our youngest daughter, Casey, graduated from college the next year, I would file for divorce. Just as planned, I served him with papers two days after her poolside graduation party. Naïvely, I had not planned for my financial future. I assumed that because we had built our wealth working side by side, and had parented four children together, he would do right by me and agree to split our assets 50/50. Instead, he went ballistic and wiped out all our joint accounts.

As the divorce process dragged on for six years, I experienced a total financial meltdown. The judge ordered spousal support, but my husband never paid it. I had to apply for financial aid to complete my master's degree. This initial setback turned out to be a blessing because I received grants that supplemented my living expenses.

Drowning in bills, I took on four jobs: tutoring at a local school, helping people prepare thesis proposals, teaching at another school, and working at the college. I still could not meet all my monthly expenses, but I knew quitting was not an option. My ex was counting on me to default on the mortgage payments so he could take the house from me. I dug in my heels. Even if I had to work six jobs, he would not take my house. It was the only thing I had salvaged from the disintegration of our marriage.

The water company came out regularly to cut the water off. The gas never was cut off because I flirted with the technician to avoid disconnection. I worried less about the electric bill and just kept candles on hand. I was so tired from working all those jobs that I didn't need light or TV when I came home at night. All I needed was sleep. Night after night I collapsed into bed and fell asleep immediately.

People who knew me on a surface level never would have believed how destitute I was, but the women in my graduate school program sensed that I was really struggling. They conveniently planned potluck suppers, and always insisted I take home large pots of extra food. I was grateful that they never questioned me or undermined my dignity.

I took a fifth part-time job as a family counselor trainee at a little Catholic school. I began to have difficulty focusing on any of my jobs because I was spread so thin. I grew so hungry that I took children's snacks out of the cubbies, praying that no one would see me. "Lord, please forgive me," I murmured as I stuffed my mouth and then my purse full of Teddy Grahams, Goldfish, and Cheerios. I was grateful my own children were grown and I did not have to fend for them too.

In a final act of desperation, I sold most of my jewelry. I kept only a couple of pieces for my daughter. This was hugely humiliating to me. I felt the buyers suspected I was selling my gold, diamonds, and emeralds to support a particular "bad habit." When I saw how little money I received for some fabulous pieces, I realized that some jewelers are poised to take advantage of women when they sense blood in the water. Now, however, I realize how unimportant jewelry is compared to the things that really matter, like sanity and self-respect.

Throughout my ordeal, I suffered from depression and anxiety, but I was fortunate to be able to work through them with my colleagues in counseling—pro bono. I did take antidepressants for a time to smooth things over. Finally, a beam of light came when my graduate program offered me a position as visiting faculty. Then I was hired for the adjunct counseling faculty at a local community college, and later as a full-time faculty member there.

Overall, it took me about six years to stabilize my life, but when I came back I was rock steady. After the divorce was finalized, I had a bucket of money from the accrued mortgage insurance, the dissipation of our liquor license (we sold five stores), four years' back payment of spousal support, and a few other windfalls. I went from barely getting by to enjoying things that I had previously taken for granted: going to the grocery store, shopping for a new outfit, getting my hair and nails done, and traveling. By then I was a size 6, down from a size 12. You might say I had missed a few meals, but I was ready for a new wardrobe and a new life that fit.

Karl had counted me out and expected me to fail, but in the end I prevailed. I have never looked back, and I never will. Now, I am traveling the world with my best friend, my daughter Casey. This time, I am using money I earned with no strings attached, and I have found my ticket to peace and genuine happiness.

757: Nancy

Clad in a full-length mink coat and wearing Prada sunglasses to conceal the panic in my eyes, I strolled into Neiman Marcus as if I belonged there. I did belong; I had long since paid my dues. My InCircle credit card was a sign of my membership in one of the nation's most elite shopping societies.

I had tucked this card away in my wallet for safekeeping. It was the only one with an open credit line that I still had. I had maxed out the others trying to stay afloat on a day-to-day basis. I had cautiously been saving it, like a bottle of fine wine, for a special occasion when I needed a little pick-me-up.

However, on this day I was not on a shopping excursion, and the occasion was not special. Desperation more aptly described my state of mind. I was not in search of the perfect cocktail dress or fuchsia suede shoes that I just couldn't live without. I was trying to meet my most basic needs. I had gone to bed hungry the night before, and I was on a mission to kill the pangs that lingered in my stomach. I sought refuge and a hot meal at the impressive Zodiac Room in Neiman Marcus.

Back in the day when my money was plentiful, I would have dined there without hesitation. I also would have picked up the tab for my entire staff. Now, however, I sat alone in the corner and discreetly tried to calculate how many more days I could afford to eat lunch there before exceeding my credit limit.

When the waiter finally came near my table, he acted as if I was invisible. I wondered if he was clairvoyant or just rude by nature. Perhaps he sensed that I was second-guessing myself as I calculated whether I could really afford to pay for the meal.

I flipped him the finger in my head and ordered the crab cake salad, praying that I had accurately guessed the balance on my Neiman's card.

As I waited for my food with sweaty palms, I sipped a cup of chicken broth and indulged in the restaurant's world-famous buttery popovers and monkey bread. I tried to remain incognito so that the other private school mothers in the room would not try to strike up a conversation or recruit me for a committee that cost money. My thoughts drifted back to a time when lunch bills were the last of my concerns. I had once lived in a world of privilege, but now I sat awkwardly among the socialites who appeared as foreigners to me. I had once had my fill of housekeepers, ball gowns, and dinners with dignitaries. That day, I couldn't have even bought a basket of groceries at Walmart.

I halted my memories, refusing to succumb to self-pity. Today I needed to feed my hunger and focus on reinvention. But as much as I tried to concentrate on my pleasant surroundings, my mind hit the rewind button again and took me back into the past. This time, I remembered how often I had given a beggar on the street a twenty-dollar bill without a second thought.

I used to ask myself how people managed to become homeless and hopeless. The notion had once seemed so pathetic to me. Now, with only $7.57 in my wallet and nothing in the bank, I understood exactly how it could happen. I silently prayed that nothing catastrophic would occur that would require cash or a working credit card. As I ended my prayer, I couldn't help but notice the crisp twenty-dollar bill that the woman sitting next to me had casually left on the table. I wished it had accidentally fallen on the floor so I could pick it up and slip it into my near-empty wallet. I wondered how much money was in her wallet.

As others engaged in animated conversations around me, I doodled in my journal. I had always had the tendency to map out my life that way. I reminded myself that apart from marrying the wrong person, I had not been irresponsible. In fact, I had even been unfairly accused of being a workaholic. The gossips didn't know I was just trying to plug the holes in a sinking ship.

I had just convinced myself that dessert was not an option when my phone rang. It was a close friend and confidante of mine. I had shared my dilemma with her earlier that morning, after I had dug the last few coins out of my change jar and found that the sum total of my liquid assets amounted to less than eight dollars. My friend was calling to get my bank account number because she wanted to wire me emergency funds.

She assured me that, in spite of the financial hardship that had lingered in my life since my divorce, God had blessed me with very special talents—gifts that would bless my life so that I in turn could bless others. She said she knew things would turn around for me if I just kept the faith. I clung to her every syllable. Her sweet words were dessert enough for me. I felt loved, and that feeling was better than crème brulée or molten chocolate cake. I thanked her for her concern, but declined her generous offer. I had a plan.

Before I left the store that afternoon, I decided to pass through the shoe department—just to make sure my fashion barometer was still working. As the saleswoman approached me, I flashed her an obligatory smile and caught my breath at the same time. I had spotted a pair of Roman inspired, orange metallic sandals. They sported a $1,495 price tag. I couldn't put them down fast enough as the math worked itself out in my head. The price of that one pair of shoes would have paid my monthly car note, insurance, and cable bill. I had spent the last of my money on those very things the day before.

To exit the store, I had to go through the accessory department. As I passed the handbags, I thought back to the Christmas when my ex-husband had bought me a $3,000 Judith Lieber evening bag from Neiman Marcus. I had insisted that he take it back. I could not be bribed. His hands had been in another cookie jar. All I wanted was his love, not a shiny consolation prize for zipping my lips. The thought occurred to me that maybe I shouldn't have spoken so soon. I could have used that purse today. I knew a great resale boutique that would have loved to add it to their collection.

By the time I got to the doors, I was roaring with laughter. I didn't care if anyone thought I was crazy. My spirits had been lifted, my stomach was full, and best of all, I was satisfied with my plans for the afternoon. Unlike some of the ladies in the lunchroom, I was not going home to a prison of ridicule and neglect, a domestic staff of traitors, or a drunk. I was not going home to a secret world of battering, where I covered my bruises for the sake of a diamond and an invitation to the Crystal Charity Ball. I had an appointment with a jeweler about a diamond of my own, and I didn't want to be late— my children's tuition was due in a couple of days.

THE POWER OF A PRAYING MOTHER: GRACE

Stanley handed me the paperwork for a prenup at our rehearsal dinner. I was in no position to absorb its content. He assured me it was no big deal, so I signed it and continued to greet our guests.

When I later uncovered my husband's numerous affairs, I prayed that God would fix him. When it became obvious that he was a functioning alcoholic, I prayed again that God would fix him. When he started hitting me, I prayed that God would make him stop. I stayed as long as I did not only for my children—I stayed because, as my parents had, I believed in marriage "till death parted us."

I forgave, forgave, and forgave some more. I had the unwavering belief that divorce was the very last resort, even in a marriage as bad as ours. I knew that God hated divorce, and so did I. However, when I heard rumors that Stanley's most recent affair (with a junior associate from his law firm) had produced a love child, I knew I couldn't take it anymore. I had been a martyr for far too long.

Even though my emotional detachment from the marriage was deliberate, I continued to hope that, after a brief separation, he would have a change of heart and come back home. Instead of coming home, my husband set out to do everything in his power to ruin me. He walked away from our boys—physically, emotionally, and financially. His detachment from them was devastating to us all. I initially tried to maintain the lifestyle the boys were accustomed to after the divorce. I reasoned that the children should not have to suffer because Stanley and I couldn't make it as a couple. I struggled to keep them in private school, but eventually just about everything else had to go.

Before I married Stanley, I had operated a successful ad agency for almost twenty years. It had been my steady and independent source of income. After our separation, the bank mysteriously called the note. I had to lay off my loyal employees, many of whom had also become my friends, and ultimately had to close the agency. I also had to sell our lovely home; I simply couldn't afford it anymore.

Before the divorce, I had the responsibility and honor of supplementing my parent's income. When my ex-husband was through with me, I could barely support myself. In spite of all this, I knew that God had his hand on me and my boys. I just needed to stay sane and have faith.

Feeling financially overwhelmed and romantically rejected, I thought that if I remarried, my problems would be solved. In all my brokenness, I became a serial dater, constantly on the lookout for a new husband. I spent far too much time focusing on this false pursuit. The dating scene wore me out, and I soon gave up. Years of therapy with a psychotherapist and the unwavering support of my mother and my wonderful friends were the necessary elements to help me to find peace and rediscover myself.

Around the time that my own nest emptied of my nearly grown children, my parents died ninety days apart, my father going first. As my mother approached the end, I was right there with her. After she passed, I was hit with the reality that I was now the only person responsible for my children. The notion was frightening and empowering at the same time.

As I went through mother's belongings, I came across letters and notes she had scribbled to God, in which she prayed for me and petitioned him for a wonderful, loving husband for me. She told him she did not want me to live alone. When she got to heaven, she must have pleaded her case in person, because I met my future husband one month after she died.

When I met Rick, I wasn't looking for a new spouse. I had finally reestablished myself financially and had successfully raised my boys alone. I was not on the hunt for a man and was indifferent to dating. Maybe my indifference was part of the attraction.

Life with Rick has turned out to be better than a fairy tale. This man tells me every morning how much he loves me and how blessed he is to have me as his wife. He cherishes me and is a man of high morals. His good looks and his professional success are added benefits.

In hindsight, the worst part of my divorce from Stanley was that he turned his back on our children when they were just little boys. I worry that this experience will taint them for life. I want so badly for them to find wonderful women to marry and be deliriously happy. While they did not have the advantage of growing up in a house with Rick and me, when they visit they see firsthand how good he is to me, and how much he loves me. I know they acknowledge this gift of love that I cherish. My boys also know they can count on one thing: until I take my last breath, I will be praying for them, just as my mother did for me.

The Road to Recovery
Pastor Joyce Reece Kitchen, LCSW/Co-Founder Sistering; Emmanuel-HM Turner AME Church

If we live long enough, sooner or later most of us are going to have our hearts broken. This should not be the end of the world. The relationship may have died, but you are still alive, even if you are severely wounded. Instead of being a coconspirator in sabotaging your livelihood and happiness, take responsibility for improving your life. You can either go through the inevitable trauma of divorce, or you can grow through the inevitable trauma of divorce. To do this successfully, you must a have plan for recovery.

As the old saying goes, "If you fail to plan, then you plan to fail." Recovery is defined as the process by which we examine what happened, formulate a plan, and become an active participant in our own healing. Our examination must be inclusive of ourselves, our spouses, and the relationship. During the examination, we sometimes find that we bear more responsibility for our brokenness than we initially acknowledge.

In order to recover from a heartbreak there are five critical supports needed:

1. **A Relationship with God**
   Your relationship with God allows you to know that there is a force in the universe that will never leave you or forsake you, no matter what happens in your life. It also allows you to be confident, knowing that any

situation in your life can be changed from an obstacle to an opportunity. Anything that you survive can transform a test into a testimony.

2. **A Support Group**
These are safe people, people who allow you to be fully yourself and fully human. They can listen to you and support you while reserving judgment. They can tell you that what you are doing is wrong or unhealthy without making you feel that you as a person are wrong, unworthy, or a failure. They will speak the truth to you in love, and that truth will help you obtain your freedom from negative situations. After years of working with women individually and in groups, I've witnessed firsthand the healing power of relational support.

3. **A Willingness to Grieve the Things You've Lost**
Too many times we try to "get over" things, but in true recovery you will learn that the only way out is through. This requires that we face our pain, feel our pain, and process our pain—all so that we can eventually be freed of our pain. Many fail to see the need to grieve a bad marriage as a loss. Even when leaving is the only answer, it still represents loss: the loss of dreams for the future, and often the loss of love. By giving ourselves permission to grieve, we minimize the amount of time needed to heal and increase the odds of our successful recovery. During the grieving process, we often find out that we didn't function solely as the victim because we were sometimes part of the problem. It is imperative that you work on yourself so you don't continue to repeat the same problem.

4. **The Ability to Hope**

   Faith can be defined as the ability to believe without seeing. In recovery from heartbreak, it becomes mandatory that we believe in our healing before we can either see or feel it. Being able to do this allows us to move forward and into a future that may have less material things, but provides true peace, which is more than the absence of chaos. True peace is the ability to have joy and faith even in the midst of the storm.

5. **A Commitment to Do the Work**

   Instead of using people, places, things, or vices to anesthetize the pain, we must focus on eliminating its source. One of the most difficult things to do when we are in pain is to refrain from reaching for someone or something to soothe it. When we allow ourselves to be distracted by external factors, we delay our recovery. The relationship has taken enough of our life—we can't afford to lose any more time.

No one will ever love you more or respect you more than you love and respect yourself. So allow what you've been through to transform you into who God created you to be.

Trust in the Lord with all your heart and lean not on your own understanding; in all your ways submit to him, and he will make your paths straight.
—Proverbs 3:5-6

Validate and Empower

For generations, girls have been misled and tricked into believing that if they did not get married their lives would not be fulfilling. This is a fairy tale that needs to die. Here's why: Family sitcoms from the 1950s through the 1970s showcased women with flawless hairdos who served martinis and tuna casseroles to the all-powerful father when he came home from a long day at the office. What was their reward? Often it was nothing more than a roof over their heads, a weekly allowance, and the "privilege" of running the house. They tucked their professional dreams away in their apron pockets and took on whatever identity and accolades their husbands afforded them.

As a baby boomer, I was not a contemporary to Donna Reed or the ficticious June Cleaver of TV land, but I did come of age at a time when young girls aspired to be a teacher but not a principal, a nurse but not a doctor, a court reporter but not a judge, the First Lady but definitely not the president. In the new millennium, however, women like Oprah Winfrey and Hillary Clinton have proved that anything is possible. Women are now shaking things up and achieving revolutionary results, attaining the once-unattainable, and making their professional dreams a reality. In doing so, they are paving the way for other women to follow.

But not everyone is happy for these high achievers. Some men simply don't want their significant other in the spotlight or making more money than they do. More alarming are those women who sit on the sidelines and throw tomatoes at their enterprising female counterparts. I have cringed at times when I have overheard women make snide remarks such as, "She might be an airline pilot or a plastic surgeon, but she still doesn't have a man." I have been equally enraged to observe mothers overtly pressuring their daughters to find a husband by the time they finish college lest they face slim pickings once they graduate. Whatever happened to the saying, "A man who findeth a wife findeth a good thing"? My own grandmother circumscribed the brilliant career my mother could have had because of her own fear of living life without a man. (By the way, my grandmother was married seven times.)

Countless women have sabotaged their life dreams due to their addiction to external approval. They perpetually seek the validation of others, especially in regard to the men in their lives. I am not sure how I got there, but I used to be one of those addicts. This kind of behavior signals that one's self-esteem is in crisis and in desperate need of repair and reaffirmation. We must all learn the difficult lesson that we should never rely on other people to define us or make us feel valuable. When we do, we diminish our authentic self and diminish the impact our life has on the world. Remember, you don't need anyone else's permission to be yourself and you don't need someone else to sign off on your dreams.

Mothers, please stop pushing your daughters off cliffs and forcing them to contribute to the high divorce rate. Encourage them to naturally develop a wholesome relationship with themselves before rushing into marriage in order to accommodate your timeline for their future. Focus on teaching them how to establish a life of self-sufficiency. Show them how to build up and protect their self-esteem. Coach them to have passions beyond china patterns. Teach them to identify and utilize their gifts.

This book is filled with stories of real women who deferred their dreams, then ended up getting dumped and having to scramble to build a new life without a husband. If being a stay-at-home mom is your genuine life ambition, that's your prerogative. However, make sure that you have a plan B tucked away in your back pocket and some cash in the bank, just in case your prince turns out to be a frog. And remember, love will be all the sweeter and more lasting if we love who we see in the mirror and understand that life mates are the cherry on top of the delicious sundae we have already built for ourselves. Repeat after me: "Mirror, mirror, on the wall, I am the most sensational girl of all!" Now practice believing that.

THE GREAT ESCAPE: JULIE

I was only nineteen years old when I met Kenneth. As a young immigrant from Columbia, I thought I was so fortunate to have met an American marine who was handsome, older, and wiser. He seemed very responsible, and just being around him made me feel very safe. This sense of security was very important to me. I was broke, naïve, and scared to be in the

United States on my own and away from my family. My sense of security lasted through almost sixteen years of marriage, until his mistress made an uninvited house call.

I could not believe this bold woman would show up at our home without any regard for our two young sons or me. I felt disrespected and undervalued. Kenneth may have been the breadwinner for our family, but this did not give him a right to walk over me like a doormat. His mistress's visit was the ultimate insult and became a turning point that drained me of all the love, respect, and trust I had once had for him. It was time for me to escape from this mockery of marriage.

The love I once showered on Kenneth was replaced by my new burning desire to take control of my life. I was not an object to be used or broken. My first goal was to figure out how I could provide for our preteen sons and myself. As much as his betrayal hurt me, I put that pain to the side, bit my tongue, and remained outwardly pleasant toward Kenneth. He never suspected that I was a woman on a mission, planning my escape while cursing him under my breath.

Realizing I was uneducated, I immediately went about achieving two key things: I took courses at the local community college, and I got a real estate license. Then, playing on Kenneth's guilty conscience, I persuaded him to give me seed money to invest in the real estate market. I set out to purchase distressed properties, renovate them, and then flip them at a handsome profit. I believe Kenneth felt real estate would be nothing more than a passing fancy for me.

He was skilled with his hands, so when he was home on leave from his military tours to Iraq he would help with the carpentry on these properties. As an officer in the military, he enjoyed taking control wherever possible, so he would assert himself and manage the crew of subcontractors.

But Kenneth had misjudged me. Arrogant as he was, he thought I would always rely on him, so he didn't pay much attention to the money that was accumulating in the bank account from my "little hobby." About two years after I started dabbling in the real-estate market, I had built an impressive portfolio of properties. I had also stashed away enough money to more than support the boys and me, as well as to send money back home to help my family.

When I asked Kenneth for a divorce, he thought at first that I was bluffing. He left that day with little resistance, wearing a confident smirk on his face. When he realized that I was serious, he attempted to get me to withdraw the divorce petition. Early one morning, I called him up and—in my most seductive voice—told him he could come home. I could hear the smile in his tone. The very thought of him being so vulnerable and naive made me smile too. He said he would be home by dinner time.

When he returned to the house early that evening, the furniture, the boys, and I were gone. I left him a note that read, "You can keep the house, but it does not come furnished with a built-in family." I now own deeds to nine rental properties. I like the United States quite a lot. As they say in the military: mission accomplished.

MALIGNANT LOVE: B. RUTH

When I first discovered the lump, I jumped up and started rubbing my breast, as if I could rub the lump out of existence. My thoughts raced to my mother, who had lost her life to breast cancer. Two months from the day my fingers revealed the war going on inside my body, I was on my way to surgery to have the tumor removed.

The doctor had warned me that if the mass proved malignant, the surgeon would remove some lymph nodes to make sure the cancer had not spread. The afternoon of my surgery, my doctor told me that the type of cancer the surgical team had removed was aggressive and had grown quickly, but only the lumpectomy was necessary. Chemotherapy and radiation followed.

My church family was wonderfully supportive during this time. They showered my family and me with home-cooked meals, cards, flowers, and prayers. Seeing how attentive the church members were to me, my husband, Tyler, sarcastically told me to let "the good church ladies" take me to my appointments for follow-up treatments.

With that, he returned to his normal routine, keeping erratic work hours and dodging my treatments. But it was not the church's responsibility to take on my husband's duties. He should have been the one to sit with me during chemotherapy, to keep me from dwelling on the fact that poison was pumping through my body. I needed Tyler's love and support to reassure me that I would live through each crisis that I faced.

But Tyler was used to me being strong and independent. He had never been emotionally supportive. Now I was facing the biggest fight of my life, and this was the time to prove he understood the meaning of "for better or for worse." I needed him to pick me up on those days when my legs felt too weak and my spirit too weary to walk into treatment.

Two months after my surgery, my younger sister was diagnosed with stage four breast cancer. In between my own treatments, I drove over to help her. As her big sister, I knew it was my duty to help her as much as I could. Her children needed her as much as mine needed me. Both of us were under the age of forty. Together, we made a pact to will ourselves to live and to support one another.

Two years after my lumpectomy, I had a cancer scare with my other breast. I did not hesitate to have a double mastectomy. My breasts had served their purpose during my childbearing years, and I was not going to risk my life now for the sake of vanity.

It probably sounds crazy to be grateful for cancer, but it was a change agent that, in many ways, saved my life. It yanked back the dark veil that had been hiding the truth about my marriage—that it had been empty and doomed from the beginning. My cancer forced me to see things as they were. For a long time, I tried to rationalize away Tyler's lack of support, but my heart knew the truth. If I could not run to him for shelter during my storms, what was his real purpose in my life?

Our marriage was like terminal cancer, spreading to every emotional cell of my body, killing me slowly. There was no cure. I knew I was a role model to my daughters, and I had to protect them by demonstrating that, as a wife, I was worthy of love and affection. I did not want them to mimic the unhealthy relationship that their father and I had.

I made the decision to leave Tyler. It was not because of mutual hatred, physical abuse, infidelity, or any of the more obvious reasons for divorce. Tyler was a good person and a decent father, but a lousy husband. He perpetually put his personal passions and career before his family. He was not wired to be the protector that God calls husbands to be.

Since my divorce, people have asked me if I was reluctant to leave my marriage after having a mastectomy. Did I feel as if I was damaged goods? Did I fear that no one else would want me? The answer to all those questions is, unequivocally, no.

Today I am cancer-free and have had reconstructive surgery. My daughters have grown up in a stress-free environment, and I am living life on my terms. My dead marriage and cancer drama are buried in the past. No person, illness, or thing will ever have the power to steal my joy. I cherish every moment I live.

One Step at a Time: Natalie

I was raised by parents who had both grown up in hostile homes. They did not have the necessary skills to be nurturing role models. As a result, I grew up feeling unlovable and married a man who reinforced that belief. I was never good enough for him. He did not give me the love and respect that all human beings deserve. Instead, he chipped away at me until I was a shell of a person.

Through counseling, I found the strength to separate from and later divorce him. At first, I was depressed, overweight, and lethargic. My sister suggested that I make a change in my life by working out. Somehow, I started to drag myself to the gym three times a week. Before long, I realized that the stress was leaving my body along with the fat. In ten months, I had lost fifty pounds and discovered the self-esteem that I had never possessed before. For the first time in my life, I felt strong, self-reliant, and proud of my appearance. My journey had begun.

I decided to become a personal trainer, and found incredible fulfillment in helping others get on the road to better health and self-appreciation. I am so grateful that I have been given the opportunity to help so many people to change their lives. Over the years, I have proudly witnessed clients lose weight, gain strength, transform physiques, raise self-esteem, lower blood pressure and cholesterol, reduce stress, and even save their marriages. I am always thrilled to hear my clients say things like, "I put on a pair of pants today that I haven't been able to wear for four years!"

My advice to someone who doesn't know where to start on a fitness plan is to call a friend and go for a walk together. Encourage and support each other. Then do it again and again. Commit to one day at a time. It gets easier. I promise.

Change does not come overnight. It comes one step at a time. I believe that true power comes from within; you already have everything you need to be happy. You just have to believe in yourself and ask God to give you the strength and discernment to identify the gifts that he has given you to use for the benefit of others. Today I am grateful that I am living in my life purpose. I am honored that every day my job is to help others feel good about themselves.

How to Validate Yourself

- Learn to love yourself first. Why would you expect someone else to lavish you with love and affection when you don't find yourself attractive, loveable, or worthy of your own affection? This is not selfish, but merely an appreciation for the valuable gift of life.
- Do not play with fire. Avoid involvement with people who are not capable of loving you. Some people have so many insecurities that they will never be able to love someone else fully. Avoid people who are unable to offer a compliment, quick to anger, unable to commit, or have not healed from a previous relationship.

- Embrace your essence. We are all constantly evolving in our bodies. Gaining a few pounds is not a reason to hate yourself or to let anyone else demean you. Figure out what is causing you to eat more than you should, then commit to do something about it for the sake of your health. Above all, regardless of whether you are a size 6 or a size 16, embrace who you are and be kind to yourself.
- Honor yourself. God made you for a special purpose. Take care of your body, keep a positive attitude, and give yourself permission to make mistakes.
- Learn to set limits and boundaries for yourself and others.
- Be financially savvy. Whether you are married or single, know what is going on with your finances at all times. This will help you avoid a lot of unnecessary stress and chaos.
- Identify and cultivate your talents and gifts. Living out your purpose will make you feel good about who you are and give you the confidence to dream big and do big things. Most importantly, this will give you a sense of confidence.
- Confidence is sexy. Dig yours up and use it.
- Expect to be treated with respect. Do not lower your standards. People will not respect you if they see that you do not respect yourself.
- Be your own cheerleader. If you have something to celebrate, don't wait for others to affirm you: go for it!

Empowerment Assignment

Take inventory of your talents, gifts, and resources by listing them here:

Now consider how you might use your gifts to help another woman in need, whether in marital, medical, financial, career, faith, legal, or emotional matters.

Remember, it is more blessed to give than to receive. When you throw someone else a lifeline, you will almost always find that your blessing in the giving rivals that person's blessing in the receiving. As you mature and embrace your gifts, you will realize that we all receive assignments to help others. Make sure you heed the call to help someone else when it comes and report for duty willingly.

I will praise You, for I am fearfully and wonderfully made.
—Psalm 139:14

Setting Royal Standards

"The divorce rate would be lower if, instead of marrying
for better or worse, people would marry for good."
—**Ruby Dee, Actress**

A marriage license does not have magic powers, nor does
a diamond ring necessarily mean that you are loved,
honored, or cherished. Neither one can erase a troubled past,
provide a new identity, or guarantee a life of bliss. When a
couple enters into a marriage covenant, it is imperative
that they meet each other at the altar with their self-esteem
intact, as well as with realistic expectations and honorable
intentions. Otherwise, someone's spirit is going to be buried
along with their unfulfilled dreams.

As women, we need to learn to trust our instincts. If
someone proposes and you have misgivings, you always have
the option of saying no—even on the day of the wedding.

Few women have the courage to call off a wedding even when they know in their gut they are about to make a horrific mistake. But here is one young lady who summoned up the courage to take control of her own destiny. She ultimately avoided divorce court and all the drama that goes with it.

Stick to Your Guns: Camille

My mother became pregnant with me when she was only sixteen. Shortly after I was born, my father became a heroin addict and disappeared. Unlike my parents, I was determined to be married and give my children a traditional home, with both parents present and sober. So, instead of focusing on college and building a career after high school, I was motivated to find someone who could deliver my "happily ever after."

I hit a few speed bumps on my quest. By the time I met Michael I had a two-year-old son, Aaron, and had experienced the pain of multiple failed relationships. Michael's arrogance was initially a turnoff. However, the affluent lifestyle that his work as an attorney and real estate developer afforded him soon overshadowed my concerns. He introduced me to a world of privilege that caused me to bury my intuition right along with my dignity.

Even though Michael made it very clear that he had no intention of getting married, I convinced myself that I could change his mind. I didn't listen to what he was saying. I gambled on the fact that since he was becoming a father figure to Aaron he would want to formalize the relationship with both of us. I kept secretly flipping through bridal magazines and felt certain I would get my way eventually.

He lived in Los Angeles, and I lived in the desert. Over time, I grew weary of the nearly two-hour commute between our houses, so I didn't press the marriage issue until about two years into the relationship. In response to my appeals he would start talking about hypothetical dates for getting engaged. But the time would always come and go with no proposal, no ring, and no plans. A piece of me died with every broken promise. To retaliate, I would break up with him and date other men, even though I was miserable without him. Michael would get jealous and beg me to get back together with him. This crazy dance went on for nearly eight years.

Eventually Aaron latched on to my anxiety. He started acting up and pulling away from Michael, whom he intuitively sensed was causing my sadness and mood swings. To complicate things, out of nowhere Aaron's birth father wanted to come back into the picture. Michael took his insecurities about that out on Aaron as well. One evening I walked in on Michael shoving Aaron; that should have been a revelation. Instead I made excuses for Michael's behavior and kept pressing for marriage.

When Michael finally bought me a ring and agreed to set a date, I should have reevaluated both our motives. Nothing had really changed. The ring was nothing more than a peace offering. Armed with *Modern Bride*, I started planning a very chic wedding at the Bellagio Hotel and Resort in Las Vegas. Michael agreed to pay for everything.

A couple of months before the wedding, as we sat together watching TV, I initiated a conversation about how we would merge our households and finances. It seemed appropriate, especially since he had just bought a new house. His body stiffened, and he made it very clear that he was not planning to add me to the deed. He was not open to my decorating suggestions either. This was the same arrogance and selfishness I has sensed when I first met him.

Then I made the mistake of asking him how we would handle our wills. He told me I should hold on to my house so that, in case he died, I could pack up and move back there with *my son.* He said I would need to sign a prenuptial agreement that provided for all of his assets to be willed to his mother, niece, and nephew. At that point, I was finally listening. I knew I deserved better.

Two days later, I called off the wedding. Two days after that, I found out that I was pregnant. For all those years I had tried to justify our fornication. Now there was physical evidence of it.

The weird thing was that Michael was ecstatic about my pregnancy—even though I had broken our engagement. He said he had always wanted a baby. Michael had me just where he wanted me: pregnant and vulnerable. We were not equally yoked in education, finances, or spirituality. I had known this all along but kept crossing my fingers. I believe to this day that God had mercy on me. I miscarried. Michael did not even go to the hospital with me when I started bleeding and had to have an emergency D and C (dilation and curettage). He told me to wake him up when I got back home.

I grieved the loss of the baby even though I didn't want it under the circumstances. I grieved that I had shared my body with someone who was not my husband. I grieved that I had wasted seven years in a dead-end relationship.

As soon as I was back on my feet, I set out to reverse my near-fatal mistake. I went to the stationery store in search of a solution. When I returned to my house, I handwrote cards to each person we had invited to the wedding: *We regret to inform you that the wedding of Camille R. Smith and Michael C. Williams has been called off. We apologize for any inconvenience this has caused you and ask that you keep us in your prayers.*

I was too broken to be embarrassed. I felt whole and in control.

While I believe crime should be punished, I now have more compassion for some of the female prisoners we have jailed for committing crimes of passion fueled by various forms of abuse. Uncontrollable rage stemming from profound disappointment is something I came to understand firsthand. As a sheriff, I was licensed to keep a firearm on me at all times, and I could not afford to let my emotions spin out of control. Thank goodness my gun was not in reach when I arrived at my boiling point with Michael.

It has been five years now. The Vera Wang wedding dress still hangs in my closet. I don't mourn it; I just haven't figured out what to do with it. One of these days, I might sell it on eBay or Craigslist. When God sends me the man he wants me to have, I will honor him with a brand-new dress, the gift of my body, and a mended heart. I finally have peace, and Michael cured me of the burning desire to have a man in my life just for the sake of a diamond and marriage license. Like Maya Angelou says, "When someone shows you who they are, believe them the first time."

Even though a broken engagement is painful and under-standably humiliating, it's better than any form of abuse you've read about in this book. Even if you have mailed the invitations, nabbed the dream dress, and your mother's bridge club members have started sending gifts, don't start popping champagne if your gut tells you that this "Prince Charming" is the wrong man for you. Calling off a wedding may seem unimaginable, but if you proceed despite flashing red lights, you will live to regret your hasty decision (if you are lucky).

As you have witnessed in "Stick to Your Guns," there is such a thing as broken engagement announcements. Everyone loves Vera Wang, so don't worry about the dress. Return it, resell it, put it on eBay, or if money is not an issue, consider donating it. Send the early wedding gifts back with a classy note thanking them for their generosity and asking them for their prayers during a very difficult time in your life. Forget the glass slippers, pour yourself a glass of champagne, and congratulate yourself on your very wise decision. Even if loved ones have traveled across the country to toast you and throw rice, turn your epiphany into a celebration of truth and boldly say, *"I don't. I can do better."*

Avoid broken engagements and/or divorce by living in reality and assessing whether or not your relationship is destined for bliss or blunder. Please, do not get married if:

- You had to issue an ultimatum to get the ring.
- Your gut says no.
- You are lonely and desperate for companionship.
- You are unequally yoked and do not share the same set of values.
- You can't live up to the vows.
- You feel the need to be rescued, whether from financial chaos, a failed relationship, a dysfunctional family, or the pressure of single parenting.
- You can't connect the dots of his past or his family. Be sure you have attended a family reunion or two and some

holiday gatherings that include his extended family. Keep your eyes open and ears to the ground when you do.

- You want to marry because you want to feel secure. You must have the ability to be your own security blanket.
- You think you should be married because all your friends are married. This is not the time to be influenced by peer pressure—especially if, truth be told, not all your married friends are happy.
- You have the notion that you can "fix" him or change him once you have him. You are wrong; you can't. If you try, he'll understandably resent you.
- You want to marry for fortune and fame. Both are temporary. Marry because you love the person, not the title.
- Your biological clock is tick-tick-ticking like Big Ben. This is not a good enough reason to make your relationship permanent, and a hasty decision could end up producing a toxic environment for your future children.

To the contrary, if you are of sound mind, and your heart and your gut tell you he is the one, if you know that you know, and you have gotten a green light from a relationship counselor, then by all means—proceed! Just remember that "for better or for worse" translates "for good." Vows are not to be taken lightly, particularly when you consider that worse could mean:

- Loss of job
- Compromised health (chronic or debilitating illness, loss of limbs, excessive weight gain, mental illness, or impotency)
- Loss of confidence and motivation, depression
- Undisclosed addictions
- Difficult in-laws

- Disabled children
- Unruly stepchildren
- Uncooperative former spouses
-
-
-
-
-
-

I encourage you to fill in the blanks with for-better-or-for-worse deal breakers to consider before you say "I do." Too often, brides sabotage their marriages by focusing only on the festivities, failing to look beyond the gift registry and down the road to reality. Marriage does not guarantee perpetual bliss, but it is so worth it if you are united with someone who is committed to being a lifelong partner and friend. Love should be an educated choice, not an uninformed chore. It is not something you just fall into; you must be prepared for the entire journey. Stop, look, and listen before crossing that bridge, because—trust me—you will be tested, probably sooner than you think.

I myself am guilty of marrying in haste. I became a divorce statistic because I did not trust my intuition. It is my belief that the majority of failed marriages, mine included, occur because the couple doesn't take the time to reach a genuine level of intimacy—through friendship—before jumping into bed. Sex does not automatically equal intimacy. When sex enters the picture before marriage, judgment typically becomes foggy, biased, and distorted. I know from experience that it is very difficult to break away from a bad relationship that ignites your passions. Honor yourself with truth. Truthfulness is at the core of intimacy. Intimacy must be at the heart of a viable and thriving marriage.

It is important to do the heavy lifting before announcing your engagement. Once the buzz has started, it is going to be difficult to pry the fabric swatches and the list of caterers out of your mother's hot little hands—or yours, for that matter. Don't open up your mouth, log on to Facebook, Instagram, Twitter, or start texting until you have had a reality check. It will spare you from having to make an embarrassing retraction.

For your own sake, please consider the following before committing to marriage:

- *Child Rearing*
  Do you both want children? What is an agreeable alternative if you are not able to conceive? What is your individual and collective philosophy on child rearing if you do decide to parent?

- *Financial Matters*
  Will you combine your finances or have separate accounts? What will happen, both psychologically and financially, if one of you loses your job? How will your wills be structured? Have you disclosed your life insurance beneficiaries to one another?

- *Outside Influences*
  What are you going to do about long-term care for your aging parents? What is your philosophy on lending money to extended family or friends?

Tips from an Expert
Pastor Lucretia Facen, Pastor and Premarital Counselor

As a pastor and a counselor for couples contemplating marriage, one of the themes I've encountered over and over are the consequences of unrealistic expectations. Our romantic notions of marriage need a good dose of reality. It's too bad that so many movies and romantic sagas end with a story book wedding and two people blissfully riding off into the sunset.

What we really need to see is Cinderella and Prince Charming after they've been married for about five years, when they have three kids, a castle mortgage, and in-laws that are giving them the royal blues. Let's see them in the middle of an intense argument about money, sex, or communication—then we'd know what unhappily ever after looks like. The truth is that happily ever after takes real work, and few couples are armed with the commitment, fortitude, accountability, intimacy, and stick-to-it-ness that a successful marriage requires.

In a Christian relationship, marriage is understood in terms of a covenant. That covenant binds the couple together not solely on their own feelings but also on the strength of God's love and commitment to them. We are able to keep the vows we make in marriage because God is included in the equation. It's interesting to me, however, how few couples forge through elaborate wedding plans without first having this basic understanding. Real faith doesn't deny real problems. Before saying "I do," couples should:

- *Take their time.* This seems simple, but is often overlooked. Rushed decisions are often wrong decisions.

- *Deal with the real.* If it quacks like a duck, it's a duck. One of the questions I always ask couples when an issue arises is "Can you live with this?" The reality is that the issue isn't going away and needs to be addressed head on.

- *Focus on the marriage, not the wedding.* The wedding only lasts one day, and sometimes reality gets lost on Fantasy

Island. I personally feel that weddings should be kept simple and sincere. Put your energy into making sure you have a solid relationship that is the foundation for a solid marriage.

Those considering remarriage need counseling as much as, if not more than, first-time couples, because the odds of failure are much higher. Also, there is more ego at risk. Anyone can explain away a first marriage, but with a second and third the "failure factor" and character flaws are significantly more pronounced.

The marriage license does not give you or your intended spouse the liberty to overburden one another with insecurities or character flaws. Pay close attention to what you hear and learn about yourself and your mate in counseling, especially if the counselor expresses well-grounded warnings or points out caution signs that could be major indications of a doomed relationship. Don't dismiss the professional's reservations. Investigate, get a second opinion if necessary, and most importantly, pray until you have an indisputable sense of peace. If you allow yourself to be quiet, the answers will come. Character flaws typically manifest themselves as some combination of dishonesty, selfishness, emotional isolation, verbal abuse, emotional abuse, financial abuse, substance abuse, physical abuse, and—lest we forget—infidelity. It is not for you to judge others, but you owe it to yourself to be alert and honor yourself with a proper mate.

Before the ink can dry on the marriage license, too many brides theoretically turn it into a death certificate because from the beginning they unwittingly:

- Approach marriage as a solution to a problem.
- Allow or even encourage their husbands to run their lives. They begin most sentences with, "My husband this" or "My husband that." It is as if they suddenly are incapable of expressing their own opinion.
- Defer every decision to their husbands, thereby ensuring they are not an equal partner in the relationship.
- Close their eyes and simply hope for the best, ignoring any signs of inappropriate behavior. You should never ignore warning signs. Address them rationally and thoughtfully as they occur.
- Allow their husbands to isolate them from family and friends.
- Confuse control with submission.
- Feel that marriage validates them.

Traditional marriage vows suggest that the wife should "honor and obey" her husband. This alludes to the notion of submission, which, under ideal circumstances, is a two-way street, as both husband and wife yield to each other. Submission does not mean that you should lose your identity. Neither does submission mean that your spouse can take liberties with your resources, your psyche, or your life. You must be able to think for yourself. Remember, someone who has your best interests at heart will encourage you to have freedom of thought and will not want to harm you emotionally, physically, or financially.

The Case for Boaz

Before we bring our journey to a close I want to make the case for Boaz. Boaz was not a king, but he made a woman named Ruth feel like a queen. His concern for her well-being was genuine and he treated her with tenderness and the utmost respect. Unlike the charming princes found in fairy tales, this gentleman was a prince of a man.

Aside from being a model citizen, Boaz was ethical, compassionate, successful, generous, responsible, and kind. He also happened to be a very hard-working and successful farmer—an entrepreneur. Now I ask you, unless she is crazy, what woman in her right mind wouldn't want to marry someone with credentials like Boaz's?

But this takes patience, along with the confidence to know that you are worthy of goodness and worthy of a man like him. I believe that God made a Boaz for every woman of integrity who wants to be married and live a life of authenticity. After all, just like Ruth, in God's eyes you are special, unique, and utterly priceless. In the kingdom of God you are considered royalty, and should be treated with kindness and dignity.

I repeat, a man who finds a wife finds a good thing. For the record, Boaz did not initially tap the recently-widowed Ruth on the shoulder and ask her out on a date. Oh, he had been watching her all right, but from afar. He was intrigued by her work ethic and especially admired the loyalty and patience she showed her elderly mother-in-law, Naomi. Here's the thing—because of Naomi's wisdom, she suggested that Ruth make the first move and let Boaz know that she was available. Ruth, in turn, did so in a way that made it clear she was both virtuous and humble.

So there you are, Ruth and Boaz, a match made with heaven's blessings—no fantasy, no fairy tale, just opportunity meeting preparedness with the help of a life coach named Naomi. Ruth had known hardship and loneliness before she met Boaz, but her patience and virtue were rewarded in the end. While you are waiting on your appointed time and your Boaz, work on yourself, love yourself, and be kind to those around you. Ruth will tell you, these principles worked for her!

If you become impatient and enter into a marriage contract with someone who gives you cause to pause, trust what your instincts tell you. If you don't you may end up giving your spouse a license to destroy the person you were created to be. Unfortunately not every marriage is guaranteed a happy ending. Do yourself a favor and wait until a Boaz is in your realm. Unlike Prince Charming, he is real and definitely worth the wait.

Afterword

Confessions of a Dragon Slayer

Back From the Dead

On July 3, 2012, at around 1:30 a.m. I was awakened by a pain so severe that I could only imagine it resembled the feeling of having an ice pick thrust into your brain. I sensed something was very wrong because no matter what remedy I tried, the pain actually increased. Finally, it dawned on me that maybe it had something to do with my blood pressure. I'd never been diagnosed with hypertension, but I figured I needed to rule that out especially since both my father and my Aunt Juanita died from a stroke.

Since my ex-husband lived so close and our daughter Zoe (who was home on summer break) had spent the night there, I called him to see if he had a blood pressure cuff. When I got to his house at around 2:00 a.m., we took my blood pressure and the numbers read 235/159. I had him call my internist, who immediately instructed us to get to the ER because those numbers were far above stroke indicators.

At around 10:00 a.m., my cell phone ringer woke me up out of a fog. Zoe, who happened to be sitting at the foot of my bed, rolled her eyes at me as if to say, "I know you are not going to answer that."

Avoiding complete eye contact with her, I hastily answered the phone I had hidden under the sheets and said, "I had our meeting down for later this afternoon. Please forgive

211

me. Something unavoidable happened but I promise, I'll make it up to you. You will have my proposal by tomorrow morning." I gazed at the IV tube protruding from my left arm. I wanted to rip it out and flee to the world where I felt most comfortable and in control—working.

Later that afternoon as Zoe was driving me home, the phone rang again before we could complete the three-mile journey. "May I speak to Ms. Mars, please?"

"This is she," I answered.

"Ms. Mars, this is the nurse from Plano ER and we need you to return to the hospital."

"Did I forget something?"

"No, ma'am. The doctor is concerned, after reviewing your films again, that you may have a cerebral bleed. We need to get you into the MRI and CAT scan lab immediately and rule that out."

Cerebral bleed? Before we could make the U-turn, my mind was scanning the faces of the people I had known who had had aneurysms and had not survived or had permanent damage. Two of my friends' mothers had died suddenly in their fifties. I was in my fifties. Was this fate like the smoke-filled airplane or had I created this life-threatening dragon with all the unnecessary battles that I had waged for so long?

When the doctor and his nurse released me for a second time that day, it was not without a justifiable lecture. "Ms. Mars, never in my career have I seen someone with your symptoms and blood pressure indicators not have a stroke, a cerebral bleed, or survive for that matter. If you do not make some drastic changes to your lifestyle, I am afraid should there be a next time you won't be so lucky. You are fortunate that the severity of the headache woke you up in the middle of the night to prompt you to seek medical attention."

It was as if the velvet drape had finally been yanked back on this Wizard of Oz—the fixer, the rescuer, the bigger-than-life architect of everyone's life but her own.

No more hiding or denying the truth; coming so close to death or permanent debilitation was the cold bucket of water that was finally waking me up after a forty-year haze after Brother's death.

Now faced with my own mortality, I realized that I had completely denied what I really wanted out of life. The only thing I was certain of was that I did not want to die a premature death and I wanted to go home to Los Angeles and rescue Debbie. Debbie, as I remember her prior to the summer of 1973 tragedy, was funny, optimistic, fearless, spoke her mind, and always made her own dreams come true.

"Where do I even begin?" my journal entry read. "Instead of going after the things I really want out of life, I have been letting other people and circumstances dictate my destiny."

Even though Mommy's premonition that Dallas would be a great place to catapult my career was correct, the most important piece of the puzzle has been missing all along. I have never been happy here, not even with the fairy tale wedding, the privileged lifestyle, and big house.

Debra Lozella Mars, the truth is that no matter how many people you know, church hats you own, or chicken dinners you attend, you feel lonely, unfulfilled, and irrelevant. The doctor was right—you were lucky. If you had died in that bed from an aneurysm or stroke, it could have been days before you were found. You're lucky to be alive but you haven't been living, not for a long time. You have to own your pathetic life and either fix it or prepare to lose it."

Unlike a screenplay, there is something about a journal entry or a handwritten note that commands honesty.

There was only one person who would fully understand the head space I was in—my godmother—so I paid her a visit. I told her now that the kids were grown, there were times when I had to look through photo albums to convince myself that I had been a good enough mother. I had privately grieved over not having enough quality time with my babies because I had spent the bulk of their childhood battling over divorce, money, business. The only person who had really gotten slayed in the process was me. My body had just demonstrated how emotionally and physically exhausted I was.

I told Mom something that I had never shared with a living soul: "In some ways I felt like a counterfeit; I had buried all my pain so deep in my emptiness and pretended that I had everything under control." It had taken a lot of energy to maintain such a lie for as long as I had.

I guess our conversation really shocked her because not long after our visit, she sent me this letter:

My Dearest Debbie,

I met you as a very young, impressionable woman, full of ambition, enthusiasm, and know-how. I was impressed with you at the very beginning of our relationship. I have known you for over thirty-five years, and my esteem for you has never wavered.

Certainly there have been times when you faced circumstances that neither you nor I would have wanted for you. You have come through it all with great dignity and pride—especially with the birth of my grandson. You have weathered many storms, including single parenting, and this remains a testimony of your faith and internal strength. These are characteristics that I know your mother would be so very proud of.

You had a secure and enviable position in Corporate America. Most people would have strived for the thirty-five-year pension and ruby ring, but you had a different vision. You made a commitment to build a legacy for your children through your own entrepreneurial endeavors, in spite of marital challenges. You have rightfully earned your children's utmost respect and the love of so many who have long admired you. You are a monument to the human spirit, to what one can do with God's help, internal fortitude, and the courage to persevere.

You have shouldered so many burdens without complaining or making excuses for your circumstances. Through it all, you have always had a passion to help others. You have always come across as upbeat and empowered, so it pains me greatly to know that you hurt as deeply as you did for as long as you did. You have been a role model for many by boldly facing life for what it is versus what you had hoped it would be.

My dear girl, you have been the kind of mother that your mother was to you. You grew up in a very loving environment. Your parents loved you dearly and you have upheld their honor by being who you are and by what you have done for so many.

Always remember, let the dead past bury its dead.

I admire that you have not held grudges and that you have forgiven liberally. I am praying for you always and I know that great things lie ahead for you. It remains my privilege to claim you as my daughter.

I love you always. Live on!

Mom

It's Just Stuff

An earnest conversation with my son came on the heels of this letter. The process of rediscovery was not accomplished by the wave of a magic wand but began by stepping up to his

215

challenge. One day he stared me in the face after the medical scare and said, "Mom, if you want to be home so bad why don't you stop dreaming about it and just do it? No disrespect but honestly, I am tired of you telling us that this is our last Christmas in Dallas. Yeah, right!"

He was right. I had been whining about moving back to LA for all of his life and it was rather hypocritical that I had lingered in the world of "if only" for as long as I did. Looking into his big brown eyes was like staring into Brother's face. It was as if he was telling me to choose life, or be dead like the uncle he never met. It was time to get radical and become fully engaged in the process of living.

"I remember this! This was Alex's first art project in school." I studied the ugly clay bird that stirred up fond memories of my young son starting school. Then I saw the poem he wrote me in seventh grade: "My Mom the Jungle Cat"—the pride of receiving it was offset by the guilt of not living up to it. I tossed the clay bird and kept Jungle Cat, vowing to live up to the warrior that my son had sensed in me when he was only twelve years old.

Materialism had held my plans to relocate hostage for far too long. Summoning up the courage to downsize, I hired an estate sale company. My instructions were as concise as if I were managing a client project. I told them to sell everything as if I were dead. Three weeks later, there were people at my door in a line that extended down the street. I had so much to sell that to this day, I can't even tell you what I sold. Unfortunately, because there was so much to be priced, tagged, and displayed during the staging period, I missed the opportunity to make sure that we were not just giving things away.

The first afternoon, I snuck into the house just to see how it was going.

"This is a lot of nice stuff. Who died?" I overheard one of the customers say.

Although I had facetiously told the sales team to liquidate as if I was deceased, to actually witness complete strangers rifling through my meticulously collected treasures and then have someone inquire about my death was sobering, particularly in light of my recent medical emergency. I was doing precisely the right thing at the right time and of my own volition.

Despite under-pricing the majority of the sale, I still made a significant amount. It was enough money to pay cash for quite a few renovations. I am told that over 1,000 people passed through in a three-day period. After the estate sale, I put my business on pause and took on the final repairs, downsizing, staging, and relocation like I was on a corporate payroll.

I still needed more money to complete all the updating and also to bridge the gap for living expenses, so I dug deeper for solutions. I even sold off part of my coveted Santa collection and my fine jewelry. I was on a mission and nothing was going to stop me; not even unscrupulous contractors I encountered.

In the end, I had three additional private sales for friends that were followed by two final public garage sales. I even pulled out my secret weapon and provided free gift-wrapping services at the last garage sale.

When Debbie's Ark sold in November 2014 after only being on the market for four days, I knew that it was time for me to run into my destiny. Thankfully, the house closed exactly when it did because when the proceeds were wired into my account I was down to my last few dollars. Whew!

Let's Get this Party Started!

As I neared moving day from the house to a transitional condo, I had very little help, which made me nervous. A very dear friend and several of her family members, along with a few other acquaintances, came to help. While they served from a place of compassion and genuine concern, I made sure that everyone left with some of my former treasures. Ironically, I gifted them the most expensive things that did not sell in the estate sale—from crystal to Henredon furniture. These emotional anchors couldn't weigh me down anymore.

When I vacated the premises at midnight per the contract, I even ended up tossing silver-plated chafing dishes, lead crystal clocks, and other wedding gifts in the dumpster in the alley as I departed. I was not getting sued for missing the midnight deadline.

I drove off in the complete darkness. I was accompanied by one faithful friend who graciously loaded down her shiny, two-seater Mercedes like Fred Sanford's junk truck. While I have never looked back, my only regret is that I failed to embrace the blessing of this almost two-decade fortress. Instead, I wasted a lot of money and energy filling it with things that I ended up selling, gifting, and in the end, tossing.

My transitional condo represented new beginnings, simplicity, and financial freedom. For the first time in almost twenty years, it was as if my brain turned back on and my stress vanished. I was no longer preoccupied with money matters or the enormous responsibility of managing a massive household alone. My initial plan was to: pay off the bills, live in the condo for about a year, and then relocate back to Los Angeles.

About four months into my lease and just as I was putting the finishing touches on the décor, I received an early morning call from a childhood friend in Los Angeles. She said there was a large house in my old neighborhood that was going on the market as a rental in two days. She was in the midst of a break-up with a long-term boyfriend and was wondering if I might be interested in leasing it together.

There was no time for me to fly out and do a walk-through, so after looking at it on the internet, I asked my nephew to proxy and represent me at the realtor meeting the next day. Understanding my fashion fetish, my friend warned me that while she felt it was a great house, the closets were very small. That gave me a cause to pause.

Conflicted, I quickly got off the phone, seeking the calming effect of water. Since I didn't have a beach nearby, I did the next best thing and jumped in the shower to try and sort things out. As the beads of water refreshed me, I started trying to envision how I would store my pared down hat and shoe collection.

As I tried to focus, I heard the Holy Spirit say to me "Debbie, I am sending you a helicopter and you are worried about where you are going to hang your clothes?"

I had everything I had prayed for and I was about to blow it. I jumped out of that shower dripping wet and called my friend back and asked her to please make an offer right away. We were approved within four days and miraculously the house never went on the market.

Giddy Up!

Finally, I was headed back to the beach, but I never had imagined that my best friend, Marshilia, would not be joining me there for routine visits. Just as cryptically as my mother had instructed me to go to Dallas, as Marshilia unexpectedly struggled to talk on the phone, she encouraged me to make the reverse commute and go back to Los Angeles.

Unlike Mommy's seven-year battle, cancer claimed Marshilia's life in four months. She died peacefully, surrounded by her loving family exactly one day before I could board the flight for what would have been our final goodbye. I returned home from her funeral numb and with no downtime to think about the couple weeks of packing that lie ahead.

The morning of my departure I returned to Frito-Lay World Headquarters and took a picture of me confidently giving a Queen's iconic wave. And why not? I had kicked down a few walls—racial, gender, and entrepreneurial disparities and I had created a little magic in the world of marketing.

My next stop was to swing through the old neighborhood to have a parting view of my Ark. Before I pulled away from what I had thought was my consolation home, I felt like I had been released from the emotional prison I had built. I also felt like I had hit the lotto when I double checked my bank account balance on my cell phone. Yes, I had a bright future that awaited me indeed. Giddy up, Caligirl!

The defining moment of my exit came when I drove past my ex-husband's house before heading to the airport. The letter I slipped in his mailbox was a manifestation of my complete release of hurt, disappointment, and betrayal. The internal war was finally over and I had emerged victorious, especially thinking about the two phenomenal children we had brought into this world.

Focusing on the silver lining, I drove off feeling like a victorious peaceful warrior.

From the moment I entered Love Field, I shamelessly told everyone who would listen that I was going home! I even told the pilot as I danced on the plane that he was carrying precious cargo so please fly the plane without incident. Yep, Debbie was back!

As the plane took off, I reached into my purse and read the promise one more time. I couldn't believe it, my dream really was coming true!

Sept 3, 1980
Dear Deb,
I am delighted you decided to make yourself content until something opens up for you in Los Angeles. You are very wise I think. Many times in life we want things to happen right now, but they don't. Sometimes waiting brings better results. Someday we will all be together again."

Love you,
Mommy

Home Sweet Home

Have you ever made a decision that you just knew that you knew that you knew was the right thing for you? Well, that's how I feel about going home. I found complete confidence in my decision when I gave myself permission to fail. I rationalized that if I didn't like LA, I could always leave again but this time of my own choosing.

I don't worry about gas prices, traffic, or anything else that my hometown is criticized for because nothing can replace the joy and contentment I feel every single day, knowing that I am surrounded by those who know me and love me best.

So far, every day is a new exciting adventure—whether it is meeting someone new, exploring a new restaurant, going to a sorority meeting, or taking a new route to the beach. No more life-threatening stress levels. Blood pressure down. The fat is melting—no dieting, just peace of mind.

No more lingering where I don't want to be. Now I chase joy every single day. Sometimes I find it in the simplest things: a glass of fresh-squeezed lemonade; a steaming cup of coffee with white chocolate macadamia nut creamer; a slobbery kiss or hug from one of my adorable six great nieces, or Tuesday Taco night with high school and college friends.

People have been telling me ever since I moved home how great I look or how happy I seem to be. They say I radiate peace and contentment. Now when I look I the mirror, I can see it too. I am grateful that I was given another chance to live out my destiny and, trust me, this time I'm not wasting any borrowed time by holding grudges or being terrified by the "what if." I have chosen to live fully in the "why not?"

My first Thanksgiving back home was filled with family, food, and nonstop laughter. I prepared the turkey and there were no leftovers. I could feel the spirit of my brother, father, and mother joining us at the dinner table. It was as if my mother's letter had come to life. She was right—I did move just at the perfect time and we were all together again in spirit.

As we washed what was left of Mommy's bone china with lots of TLC, I looked out the kitchen window which faces my childhood backyard. I could imagine the red metal swing set with my thick braids swaying in the wind. My childhood memories are filled with magical moments like Christmases, birthday parties and everything else that puts a smile on a child's face and makes them feel safe and loved.

Beyond the magical moments and sweetness, life is a journey peppered with unpredictable and sometimes unthinkable battles. Some life situations are simply inconvenient nuisances; others are ... dragons, and there are all kinds of them. They don't all rear their ugly heads in marital or relationship settings.

My new-found philosophy is quite simple: You either tame a dragon (by taking away its power to incite fear or chaos in your life) or you slay a dragon (by eradicating its presence from your life altogether). What are your dragons? Not to be Debbie Downer, but trust me, for as long as you live — and I hope you will live a long time —there will always be something, some dragon that could potentially derail your dreams and temporarily rob you of your joy. Should that time arise, hone the power of the dragon slayer within. Always trust your gut and defend your honor with dignity and confidence. Then enjoy the rest and reprieve and never back down from defending the life you deserve.

Life is not a fairy tale but some pretty amazing things can happen if you will only believe in the power of favor, grace, and, yes, miracles.

Just like Dorothy, I clicked the heels of my cowgirl boots three times and, *poof*, they magically turned into flip-flops and I wound up right in my own backyard where my life began. I love my life now and I love the woman my mother, Jo Lozella, and godmother, Evelyn, always knew I would become.

So there you are, little Debbie did have a very happy ending after all. She learned to love, and honor herself, no matter the situation she finds herself in. She is cherished by her children, her sister, nieces, nephews-in-law, great-nieces, stepchildren, and a host of other family members and friends.

Most importantly, she cherishes herself enough to practice self-care, fully understanding that not all of life's battles are meant to be fought. She also hopes that you will now believe that the magic of life begins with the ability to live in truth, with wisdom, forgiveness, humility, peace, and always with a sprinkling of laughter. She is living the Happier Ever After after all and beckons you to join her.

Dare to reign and take someone with you.

Wisdom is the REWARD of EXPERIENCE and should be Shared.

Divorce is a death, no matter a person's social status. However, unlike the death of a spouse, people are not lining up to bring you flowers, a chicken dinner or a roll of stamps. Women going through an unwanted divorce are especially vulnerable and often find themselves in a state of emotional upheaval and financial devastation; both which could lead to unmanageable levels of stress and depression. Regardless of their relationship to you, I challenge you to develop a greater awareness and sensitivity for the newly minted divorcee.

Starting Over (Your Sister's Keeper)

There are some extreme cases where a woman has fled in a moment's notice to save her life and the lives of her children. There are more subtle situations that simply challenge their self esteem. All of are in need of extended support even if just a kind word or supportive smile.

Here are some ways you can support women going through divorce:

225

- Throw her a "divorce shower" especially if she has had to walk or run away from everything which necessitates assembling a new home.
- Child care support. Offer to baby sit or assist with car pool
- Organize a food chain
- Take her comedic DVDs or an upbeat play list
- Bring her groceries and cook with her
- Buy her a gift certificate for a massage, mani or pedi
- Purchase a gift certificate for a home organizer or cleaning service.
- Take her to lunch or dinner and if you are married consider including your husband or significant other so she knows you are both still in her life
- Introduce her to your friends, especially friends who have gone through divorce and help her develop a circle of empathetic supporters
- Bring her flowers to brighten her day
- Write her a note of encouragement that she can refer back to (do not text or email)
- Buy her a whimsical or inspirational gift
- Be a reliable and confidential ally to her; do not judge her thoughts or actions just listen if she needs to talk
- Accompany her to church or invite her to join your church
- Offer to take up a hobby with her

Note: If it is a physical gift, take the time to wrap it yourself or have it gift wrapped and don't forget to add a note of encouragement!

Whether you are going through divorce or someone you care about, here are some resources that will hopefully prove helpful in the healing and restoration after divorce.

DIVORCE RESOURCES

Apps:

1. DivorceForce is an app and free online community committed to empowering those affected by divorce.

   - https://www.divorceforce.com

2. Join over 500,000 others who use Balanced to stay motivated and focused on what's really important in life.

   - http://balancedapp.com

3. Divorce Rebuild Life helps you to move forward in life after divorce.

   - https://itunes.apple.com/us/app/divorce-rebuild-life/id375280487?mt=8

4. Sesh matches you with an expert life coach and connects you via live video chat and text messaging.

   - https://joinsesh.com

5. Ask a Psychologist provides quality advice from real people. 50% of all profits are donated to The ALS Association charity.

   - https://itunes.apple.com/us/app/ask-psychologist-psychologist/id927932286?mt=8

Websites:

1. **Divorce 360**is a website that provides **help**, **advice** and **community** for people contemplating, going through or recovering from divorce and the issues around it - custody, child support, alimony, etc.

   - http://www.divorce360.com

2. The goal of this next site is to help women survive divorce and rebuild their lives.

    - http://www.womansdivorce.com

3. The mission of First Wives World is to empower women through divorce and other life challenges with positive support, resources and community.

    - https://www.firstwivesworld.com

EMOTIONAL ABUSE

Websites:

1. Springtide Resources is a charity that develops and implements programs aimed at responding to the prevention, intervention and educational needs of those working toward ending violence against women and their children.

    - http://www.springtideresources.org/resource/ emotional-abuse-women-male-partners-facts

2. This Is a War

    - http://thisisawar.com/AbuseEmotional.htm (Website under construction)

3. This site is dedicated to the recognition and prevention of verbal abuse in homes, schools, and work places.

    - http://www.verbalabuse.com

Campaigns:

1. **"Words can be Weapons"** Campaign uses social media to raise awareness of verbal abuse.

- Words Are Weapons Campaigns: https://social.ogilvy. com/words-can-be-weapons-campaign-uses-social-media-to-raise-awareness-of-verbal-abuse/

2. **The Good Men Project** set out to start an international conversation about what it means to be a good man in the 21st century. There are stories of abuse and relationships.

   - The Good Men Project: http://goodmenproject.com/ethics-values/emotional-abuse-invisible-train-wreck-fiff/

Articles:

1. This study aimed to investigate the moderating roles of gender and age on emotional abuse within intimate relationships.

   - Studies on Emotional Abuse and Domestic Violence: http://www.ncbi.nlm.nih.gov/pmc/articles/PMC3876290/

2. "Emotional abuse is considered common, but statistics are hard to come by, since it's difficult to legally document demeaning behavior until it involves a threat and because so many are unsure about what it is. According to the National Coalition Against Domestic Violence, roughly 85 percent of domestic violence victims are women."

   - Signs of Verbal Abuse: http://health.usnews.com/health-news/health-wellness/articles/2013/10/03/the-telltale-signs-of-verbal-abuse

3. "People victimized by verbal abuse in marriage, or other verbally abusive relationships, don't want to give up easily. There is love or money (or both) at stake, and they could feel that the sacrifice of walking away is too great.

Victims of verbally abusive relationships most want to know how to respond to verbal abuse and how to stop verbal abuse."

- Getting Out of Emotionally Abusive Relationships: http://www.healthyplace.com/abuse/verbal-abuse/5-ways-of-dealing-with-verbally-abusive-relationships/

Empty Nest Syndrome

Websites:

1. This website gives advice on how to cope with an empty nest after divorce by getting prepared, becoming a people person, rekindling forgotten passions, using the phone and loving yourself.

  - http://divorce.lovetoknow.com/Empty_Nest_After_Divorce

2. This is an online discussion board for people who are going through empty nest syndrome.

  - http://www.dailystrength.org/c/Empty-Nests/support-group

Programs:

1. Natalie Caine M.A. is the founder of Life in Transition, which provides **Empty Nest Support Services**. She helps empty-nest families through the joys and challenges of a new life chapter. Her website has tips and counseling services.

  - http://www.emptynestsupport.com

The Financially Abused

Websites:

1. "Financial abuse is one form of domestic abuse. Withholding money, stealing money and restricting the use of finances are some examples of financial abuse. To figure out if your partner is financially abusing you, think about how you are being treated by answering the following questions."

   • http://www.womenslaw.org/laws_state_type. php?id=14107&state_code=PG

2. National Credit Care focuses on details and offers options to clients that have gained an understanding for being known for their creative and customized credit solutions.

   • http://www.nationalcreditcare.com

3. Credit Repair is dedicated to helping you develop a healthier relationship with your credit.

   • https://www.creditrepair.com

4. The Credit Info Center has tips on getting the best credit card, how to rebuild your credit, ordering your credit reports and scores, budgeting your money, and legal advice when dealing with creditors and collection agencies.

   • http://www.creditinfocenter.com

STRESS MANAGEMENT, DEPRESSION, AND SUICIDE PREVENTION

1. Stress Management

Apps:

- Pacifica is an app that gives you holistic tools to address stress, anxiety and depression based on Cognitive Behavioral Therapy, mindfulness, relaxation, and health.

  - https://www.thinkpacifica.com

- Reduce, manage, and learn about stress in your life with the Calm in the Storm app.

  - http://calminthestormapp.com

Severe stress can bring upon a panic attack, which often mimics a heart attack.It's important to know the difference:

Panic Attack vs. Heart Attack

- Heart disease in women is often mistaken for panic attack with shortness of breath, anxiety, palpitations and indigestion.
  - ✔ Chest pain and difficulty breathing are common symptoms in both panic attack and heart attack as they trigger the body's "fight or flight" response, but these are also signs of ischemia - a lack of blood flow to the heart muscle.
- Only by having testing beyond the standard EKG can a correct diagnosis be made.
  - ✔ Some tests of the tests available to diagnose a heart attack are an electrocardiogram, blood tests, stress tests, electron beam computed tomography, magnetic resonance imaging, and angiography.

- http://www.womensheart.org/content/heartdisease/
panic_attack_or_heart_attack.asp

How to tell the difference between an anxiety attack and a heart attack?

If you are having a hard time telling the difference between the symptoms associated with an anxiety attack and those of a heart attack, here are some things to watch for:

- Anxiety attacks generally produces more symptoms than just those similar to a heart attack.
- Anxiety attacks generally don't cause people to pass out.
- Anxiety attacks can cause hyperventilation, which can cause symptoms similar to those of a heart attack.
- While anxiety attacks can upset the stomach and make it feel like you need to vomit, most people generally don't.
- Calming yourself down can end an anxiety attack, which will cause the cessation of anxiety attack symptoms.

  - http://www.anxietycentre.com/anxiety/faq/heart-attack-or-anxiety-attack.shtml

Articles:

- Divorce and Anxiety/Panic Attacks

  - http://www.divorce360.com/divorce-articles/
help/self-help/is-divorce-causing-anxiety-panic.
aspx?artid=758

2. Depression

The depressioncheck M3 app is a state-of-the-art, research validated screen that in 3 minutes assesses your risk of depression, bipolar and anxiety disorders.

- https://itunes.apple.com/us/app/depressioncheck/id398170644?mt=8

I am – Daily Positive Reminders is an app that sends daily affirmations that help rewire our brains, build self esteem and change negative thought patterns.

- https://itunes.apple.com/us/app/i-am-daily-positive-reminders/id874656917?mt=8

3. Suicide Prevention

Facebook recently launched a helpful resource for suicide prevention:

- https://www.facebook.com/help/594991777257121/

Lifebuoy is an interactive, self-help promoting app designed to assist suicide survivors as they normalize their lives after recent attempt.

- https://itunes.apple.com/us/app/lifebuoy-suicide-prevention/id686973252?mt=8

National Suicide Prevention Lifeline: 1-800-273-8255 (TALK)

- www.suicidepreventionlifeline.org

SUBSTANCE ABUSE HELP

1. The National Institute on Drug Abuse aims to advance science on the causes and consequences of drug use and addiction and to apply that knowledge to improve individual and public health.

- https://www.drugabuse.gov

2. Substance Abuse and Mental Health Services Administration (SAMHSA's) mission is to reduce the impact of substance abuse and mental illness on America's communities.

   * http://www.samhsa.gov

3. The goal at **Recovery.org** is to connect people and their families with the information and resources to help them recover from substance abuse and behavioral disorders.

   * http://www.recovery.org

4. **Addiction Resource Guide** is an internet company whose mission is to help professionals and consumers find resources for dealing with addictive problems.

   * http://www.addictionresourceguide.com

   Drug Abuse Hotline: 1-800-959-7812

DOMESTIC VIOLENCE

Websites and Campaigns:

1. **National Resource Center on Domestic Violence (NRCDV's)** mission is to strengthen and transform efforts to end domestic violence.

   * http://www.nrcdv.org

2. The vision of **Nation Coalition Against Domestic Violence (NCADV)** is to create a culture where domestic violence is not tolerated; and where society empowers victims and survivors, and holds abusers accountable.

   * http://www.ncadv.org/need-help/resources

3.) **NO MORE** is a unifying symbol and campaign to raise public awareness and engage bystanders around ending domestic violence and sexual assault.

- http://nomore.org

Hotlines:

The National Domestic Violence Hotline: 1.800.799. SAFE (7233) http://www.thehotline.org

National Sexual Assault Hotline: 1.800.656.HOPE (4673)

National Center on Domestic Violence, Trauma & Mental Health: 1-312-726-7020 ext. 2011

Futures Without Violence: The National Health Resource Center on Domestic Violence: 1-888-792-2873

INFIDELITY

1. **Truth About Deception** is a group of scholars, scientists, and working professionals interested in sharing information about why people lie to, and cheat on, those they love.

- https://www.truthaboutdeception.com

2. The **American Association for Marriage and Family Therapy (AAMFT)** is the professional association for the field of marriage and family therapy.

- http://www.aamft.org/iMIS15/AAMFT/

Legal

1. American Bar Association Commission on Domestic Violence aims to increase access to justice for victims of domestic violence, sexual assault and stalking by mobilizing the legal profession.

   • www.abanet.org/domviol

2. The **Battered Women's Justice Project (BWJP)** has worked to improve the civil and criminal justice system's response to intimate partner violence (IPV).

   • 1-800-903-0111

   • www.bwjp.org

Eating Disorders

1. Recovery Warriors – Wonderful Pro recovery site with podcasts, resources, and online directory of Eating Disorder professionals.

2. ED Referral – Not all therapists know how to treat eating disorders, and not all know how to recognize binge eating disorder. If you are looking for someone who understands your needs, this is a great resource.

3. National Eating Disorder Association– A non-profit group aimed at healing EDs. Lots of inspirational stories, as well as posted research and events.

4. Binge Eating Disorder Association– An organization aimed at helping people heal from Binge Eating Disorder using a non-diet approach

5. <u>Pale Reflections</u>– Online support Community

6. <u>National Association of Anorexia and Associated Disorders</u>– A non profit that provides free support groups as well as informational pamphlets and literature.

7. <u>Association of Professionals Treating Eating Disorders</u>– This is primarily a Bay Area resource that provides low fee treatment for EDs.

8. <u>Health at Every Size</u>– A group aimed at improving your self love and body acceptance as well as encouraging healthy eating and exercising habits without dieting or idealizing a different body size or shape.

9. <u>The Body Positive</u>– An organization aimed at love and positivity toward yourself and your body. It's aim is to help you gain self love, happiness and good health without telling you that you need to diet in order to get those things.

10. <u>Beauty is Contagious</u>– Not a resource, but a wonderful Tumblr with lots of images of beautiful bodies in every size and shape.

11. <u>Overeaters Anonymous: Newcomers</u>

    - <u>https://oa.org/</u>
    Overeaters Anonymous
    No matter what your problem with food — compulsive *overeating*, under-eating, food addiction, anorexia, bulimia, binge eating, or overexercising

About the Author

D. L. Mars is a former corporate marketing executive and a successful entrepreneur (Gifted by Dezyn, Inc.). She is the founder of Women In The Game, a mentoring organization dedicated to helping women reestablish their self-confidence and financial security after life-altering challenges. A native of Los Angeles, she graduated with honors from the University of Southern California (BS) and the University of Wisconsin-Madison (MBA). She is the grateful mother of two adult children.

Contact Information

Contact the author at: dlmars@deathofafairytale.com

To purchase additional copies of this book and shop
in our Dare to Reign Boutique visit us at:
deathofafairytale.com

Website blog https://daretoreign.wordpress.com/
Instagram https://www.instagram.com/daretoreign/
Facebook https://www.facebook.com/daretoreign
Twitter https://www.twitter.com/daretoreign